CRICKET QUIZ BOOK

Also by Mansel Davies and Ian Thomson in Sphere Books:

TENNIS QUIZ BOOK
FOOTBALL QUIZ BOOK
GOLF QUIZ BOOK

Cricket Quiz Book

Ian Thomson
and Mansel Davies

SPHERE BOOKS LIMITED

SPHERE BOOKS LTD

Published by the Penguin Group
27 Wrights Lane, London W8 5TZ, England
Viking Penguin Inc., 40 West 23rd Street, New York, New York 10010, USA
Penguin Books Australia Ltd, Ringwood, Victoria, Australia
Penguin Books Canada Ltd, 2801 John Street, Markham, Ontario, Canada L3R 1B4
Penguin Books (NZ) Ltd, 182–190 Wairau Road, Auckland 10, New Zealand

Penguin Books Ltd, Registered Offices: Harmondsworth, Middlesex, England

First published by Sphere Books Ltd 1988
10 9 8 7 6 5 4 3 2 1

Printed and bound in Great Britain by
Richard Clay Ltd, Bungay, Suffolk

1 The 1987 World Cup tournament

1. Who took the crucial wicket of England's captain, Mike Gatting, with his first ball of the 1987 World Cup Final in Calcutta? *Allan Border*

2. Who displayed a superb mastery of the 'sweep' shot against India's spin bowlers, scoring a match-winning 115 for England in their World Cup semi-final in Bombay? *Graham Gooch*

3. Who was England's most successful bowler in the 1987 tournament, his 13 wickets including 4 against India in their semi-final clash? *Eddie Hemmings*

4. Who was the Zimbabwe vice-captain and wicket-keeper who scored 141 runs against New Zealand, at the time the third highest score in the tournament's history, as well as featuring in a competition record eighth-wicket partnership of 117, yet still finished on the losing side?

5. Who subsequently scored 181 against Sri Lanka out of his side's record-breaking 360–4, establishing a new individual record for the competition? *Viv Richards*

6. Who hit West Indian fast bowler Courtney Walsh for a six off the last ball of the match to earn Pakistan a one-wicket victory in their Group B game at Lahore? *Abdul Qadir*

7. Who scored 103* off 85 balls received, his first century in one-day internationals, as India raced to 224–1 for a straightforward victory over New Zealand in their Group A game at Nagpur? *Sunil Gavaskar*

8. Who claimed an all-bowled hat-trick for India in New Zealand's total of 221–9 in the above match, the third recorded hat-trick in a one-day international? *Chetan Sarma*

Note
Throughout this book, the asterisk is used, in accordance with convention, to indicate 'not out'.

9. Who took 5 Pakistan wickets for 44 runs in the 1987 semi-final match at Lahore, on his way to a total of 18 wickets for the tournament which put him one ahead of Imran Khan as the 1987 competition's leading wicket-taker? CRAIG McDERMOTT

10. Who top-scored with 75 runs in the 1987 World Cup Final, profiting from some wayward English seam bowling and winning himself the Man of the Match award?
DAVID BOON

2 Current Players with their second County

1. Who is the Essex slow left-arm bowler who played for Gloucestershire between 1975 and 1984?

2. Who is the Gloucestershire batsman who played for Yorkshire between 1976 and 1983?

3. Which county did Lancashire wicket-keeper Chris Maynard represent between 1978 and 1982?

4. Who played for Northamptonshire between 1966 and 1983, before transferring his allegiance to Leicestershire?

5. With which county did Middlesex wicket-keeper Paul Downton commence his first-class career in 1977?

6. Who is the Nottinghamshire batsman who played for Gloucestershire between 1979 and 1983?

7. Who played for Warwickshire between 1966 and 1978, and then joined Nottinghamshire?

8. Who played for Hampshire between 1966 and 1984, before transferring to Surrey?

9. Who played for Sussex from 1974 to 1985, prior to joining Lancashire?

10. Who is the Worcestershire bowler who played for Lancashire between 1980 and 1984?

3 All-Rounders in Test cricket

1. Which player in January 1987 dismissed Sri Lanka's Rumesh Ratnayake, to become the second man after Ian Botham to score 3,000 runs and take 300 wickets in Test cricket?

2. Who is the only Englishman to score 500 Test runs and take 50 Test wickets in a calendar year?

3. Who was the first player to perform the Test match 'double' of 1,000 runs and 100 wickets for Pakistan?

4. Which all-rounder scored 201* for Pakistan against New Zealand at Dunedin in February 1973, more than the opposition's score in either innings, and followed this up with 5–49, so becoming only the second player to score a double century and take five wickets in an innings of the same Test match?

5. Which three players, an Australian, a South African and a West Indian, are the only left-handed batsmen/left-handed bowlers to have performed the Test match 'Double' of 1,000 runs and 100 wickets?

6. Which player in the 1960 Tied Test became the first man to perform the match 'double' of 100 runs and 10 wickets in a Test match, scoring 44 and 80 and having analyses of 5–135 and 6–87?

7. Who, at Trent Bridge in July 1957, scored 191* in the Third Test between England and the West Indies, and took 7 wickets for 70 in the following Test at Headingley?

8. Three members of the great Australian side that toured England in 1948 were to achieve the Test match 'double' of 1,000 runs and 100 wickets: Ray Lindwall, Keith Miller and which other player?

9. Which all-rounder in 1952 became only the second man, after Australia's Jack Gregory thirty-one years earlier, to achieve the feat of 500 Test runs and 50 Test wickets in a calendar year?

10. Who, at Old Trafford in July 1896, became the first player to score 1,000 runs and take 100 wickets in Test matches?

4 Around the Counties

1. Which former England player scored a career-best 181 in August 1984 at the age of forty-three?

2. Which county failed to win the 1984 Britannic Assurance Championship by 'just four runs', when, in the season's final game, their last man in was caught on the long-off boundary by Somerset substitute fielder, Richard Ollis?

3. Who in 1984 scored his maiden first-class century for Glamorgan, in his eleventh season with the county, and proceeded to finish the season with a total of five Championship hundreds?

4. Who, between 1947 and 1957, exceeded 2,000 runs in a first-class season on nine occasions, a post-war record?

5. Which county did Allan Border represent in 1977, scoring 15* on his only first-class appearance, a rain-restricted match against Oxford University at the Parks?

6. Who set a world record in 1920, achieved the 'double' six times between 1921 and 1928, coupling the feat with 50 catches in 1921 (a feat unique to him), and prior to his death in 1985 was the oldest surviving Test player, at ninety-two years of age?

7. Which scorer of two centuries for England, who retired in 1987 after twenty-four years in the first-class game, scored his only double century at the age of forty-one, 200 exactly against Northamptonshire in 1985?

8. Which former England batsman won the 1987 Lawrence Trophy with a century in seventy-three balls against Sussex, his solitary three-figure score in an otherwise disappointing year?

9. Who carried his bat for 33 against the 1985 Australian tourists, the first player to do so for his county since Frank Lee, 59* against the 1934 Australians?

10. Who, in the split-tour year of 1982, scored 164* for Hampshire against the Indians and followed this up with 133 against the Pakistanis?

5 *Test Cricket – Captains*

1. Who has captained his country in a record seventy-four Test matches?

2. Who captained India in forty of his forty-six Test matches, taking on the role at twenty-one years of age, the youngest player to captain any country?

3. Who played three Tests for India before becoming a citizen of Pakistan, and leading that country in its first twenty-three Test matches?

4. Who captained New Zealand in a record thirty-four successive Test matches between 1956 and 1965, during which time he led them to their first ever Test match victory, against the West Indies at Auckland in March 1956?

5. Who captained South Africa against Australia in 1969–70, their last official Test match series?

6. Who captained South Africa in ten Test matches, all against England, failing to win any of them, although having phenomenal personal success as a batsman, scoring four successive centuries?

7. Who in March 1982 captained Sri Lanka against England in their first official Test match?

8. Who took over the West Indies captaincy in 1977–78 when Clive Lloyd resigned over the 'Packer Affair'?

9. Who were the respective captains in the first Tied Test, at Brisbane in December 1960?

10. Who led Sri Lanka to her first victory in Test cricket, a 149-run win over India in September 1985?

6 One-day cricket – The Sunday League

1. Which county won the final John Player League championship in 1986, their third success in the eighteen years of the competition, a record shared jointly with Essex and Kent?

2. Which county confirmed their overall victory in the inaugural Refuge Assurance League championship, beating Northamptonshire in their last match in September 1987?

3. Who in May 1987 scored the first century in the new Refuge Assurance League, hitting 125* against Derbyshire at Derby?

4. Which outstanding batsman 'set out his stall' at the earliest opportunity in the Refuge League, playing an innings of 172 against Surrey in May 1987, during which he shared in a record Sunday League fourth-wicket stand of 219?

5. Which Glamorgan bowler, when, playing against Nottinghamshire, took the first hat-trick in the Refuge Assurance League, in June 1987?

6. Who brought the John Player League to a dramatic end in 1986, providing a sensational innings of 175* which contained a record 13 sixes?

7. Which pair followed up a double century opening partnership in the 1985 NatWest Final, with a first-wicket record of 239 in the Sunday League the next day against the same opposition?

8. Who was the only bowler to take 8 wickets in a John Player League match, recording figures of 8–26 against Lancashire at Old Trafford in 1971?

9. Who was the former Loughborough student who had a brief career with Somerset, during which he set a record with 34 wickets in the 1974 John Player League season, at a cost of 13.17 runs each?

10. Which recently retired all-rounder illustrated his value as a cricketer with a record 814 runs in the Sunday League in the 1978 season, and a record-equalling 34 wickets in 1986?

7 England v. Australia – Test miscellany

1. Who scored three centuries for England against Australia in the 1986–87 series, the first being his maiden three-figure innings in Test cricket?

2. Who in January 1987 achieved his best bowling figures in Test cricket, taking 7–78 in Australia's second innings in the final match of the series at Sydney?

3. Who scored 59 of Australia's second innings total of 142 at Edgbaston in 1985, being unluckily dismissed when a fiercely struck square-cut lobbed up to David Gower off Allan Lamb's boot?

4. Who scored 732 runs for England in the 1985 Ashes Tests, completely eclipsing Denis Compton's 1948 record of 562 runs by an English batsman in a home series?

5. Who ended the 1985 Ashes series with 3 wickets for 275 runs, the third victim, Graham Gooch, being his 200th in Test matches and his 100th wicket against England?

6. Who in 1985 became only the fourth bowler to concede over 900 runs in an Ashes series?

7. Who forced an England victory by 29 runs at Edgbaston in 1981, when taking the last five Australian wickets at a personal cost of one run in just 28 deliveries?

8. Who scored 56 runs, his highest Test innings to date, when sharing an eighth-wicket stand of 117 with Ian Botham during the unforgettable Third Test Match at Leeds in 1981?

9. Who returned to Test cricket in 1977, after a thirty-match absence, and scored 442 runs in the series against Australia, at an average of 147.33?

10. Who, at the Oval in 1977, in his only Test match for Australia, took 6 of the 12 England wickets to fall during the match, conceded only 77 runs from his fifty-seven overs, and in addition scored a career-best 46 in his only innings?

8 *County Championship captains*

1. Which cricketer, captain of his county from 1978 to 1983, played in four 'Test Trials' between 1974 and 1981, scoring a century for MCC v. Worcestershire in 1975 and captaining MCC in 1981, yet retired in 1984 without winning a Test cap?

2. Which players, captains of Kent, Lancashire, Northamptonshire, Sussex and Warwickshire respectively, all played for England against South Africa at Edgbaston in June 1960?

3. Which man, who captained his county between 1981 and 1986, was born in Bonn, West Germany?

4. Who played thirteen Championship matches for his county in 1985, none at all in 1986, but in 1987 returned to first-class cricket as captain of another county?

5. Which county captain started off the 1987 first-class season by registering 'pairs' in his county's first two home games of the season, against Warwickshire and the touring Pakistanis?

6. Who led Essex both before and after the Second World War, his first period as captain running from 1933 to 1938, and his second from 1946 to 1950?

7. Who was appointed captain of Gloucestershire for the 1961 season, a decision which led to Tom Graveney leaving the county for neighbouring Worcestershire?

8. Who, in his first season as captain, led Kent to the County Championship in 1978?

9. Who captained the last Yorkshire team to win the County Championship?

10. Who led Lancashire for five seasons between 1968 and 1972, and after a brief retirement returned to first-class cricket in 1974 as captain of Derbyshire, his new county rather tarnishing his reputation as a leader by finishing bottom of the Championship with just one victory?

9 *Test match miscellany*

1. Which England opening batsman remained on 66 for ninety minutes during his innings of 89 in the First Test at Perth in November 1982?

2. Which twenty-one-year-old made his international début in the above game, becoming England's 500th Test player?

3. When Sunil Gavaskar made his Test début in the 1970–71 series against the West Indies, scoring 774 runs in four matches, which other Indian batsman scored 642 runs in the series at an average of 80.25, including an innings of 212 in the First Test at Kingston, after India had been 75–5?

4. Who, in December 1903, became the first English wicket-keeper to make 50 dismissals in Ashes Tests?

5. Who, in January 1921, became the first English player to perform the 'double' of 1,000 runs and 100 wickets in Ashes Tests?

6. Which two specialist batsmen scored 0 and 1 in England's total of 903–7 at The Oval in 1938?

7. Who, in his first Test innings, scored a 132-minute century for New Zealand against Pakistan in February 1973, following this with 56 in quick time in the second innings, but, losing form and subsequently having to retire early from first-class cricket because of eyesight problems, never played in another Test match?

8. Who made his Test début for England at Lord's in August 1983 and, opening the batting with Chris Tavaré, was leg before wicket to Richard Hadlee from the first ball he received?

9. Who linked up with the England tour party to New Zealand in February 1984 and, because of injuries to Graham Dilley and Neil Foster, made his Test début in Christchurch, taking the wicket of Bruce Edgar with his seventh ball?

10. Who, when he made 116 against England at Faisalabad in March 1984, became only the third batsman to score three Test centuries before the age of twenty-one?

10 *Cricket records*

1. Who, in 1973, scored 1,018 runs by the 31 May, the last occasion, prior to 1988, on which 1,000 runs were scored in first-class cricket before the end of the first full month of the season?

2. Who holds a world record for scoring a century in both innings of a match on eight occasions, in addition to scoring a double century and a century, without losing his wicket in either innings, in four of these matches?

3. Who was the nineteen-year-old who in June 1985 scored 230 for Zimbabwe against Oxford University, the sixth highest score in England by a batsman making his maiden first-class century?

4. Who scored 317 runs in 230 minutes off 245 balls for New Zealand against Brian Close's XI at Scarborough in September 1986?

5. Who set a world record for the highest innings composed entirely of boundaries, 46 (ten fours and a six), when playing for England against Tasmania in December 1986?

6. Which two overseas players shared a county record fourth-wicket stand of 306, unbroken, for Glamorgan against the 1985 Australian touring team?

7. Who was the uncapped batsman, playing for Worcestershire against the Pakistani tourists in 1982, who made his highest score in first-class cricket at that time when he scored 93 out of 102 runs added while he was at the wicket?

8. Which county side totalled 616–6 declared against Oxford University in 1982, with their first four batsmen all scoring centuries?

9. Which county, playing against Warwickshire at Birmingham in 1896, scored a Championship record total of 887?

10. Which two batsmen both scored triple centuries on the same day in July 1937, one for Hampshire against Warwickshire at Bournemouth, and the other for Lancashire against Sussex, also on the south coast, at Hove?

11 *England bowlers*

1. Which bowler played in thirty-four Tests for England, straddling the Second World War years, and took 108 wickets at the abnormally high average of 39.11?

2. Who made the last appearance of his twenty-seven-match Test career at Durban in February 1914, bowing out in style with 14 wickets for 144 runs?

3. Prior to 1987, who was the only England bowler to concede over 200 runs in a Test innings when, against Australia at The Oval in 1930, he took 6–204?

4. Who took 4 Pakistani wickets in five balls at Edgbaston in June 1978, twice being denied a hat-trick, the first time when bowling a no-ball?

5. When Gordon Greenidge scored 214* against England at Lord's in 1984, who shared the Man of the Match award with him, taking 8 wickets in West Indies first innings?

6. Who made his Test début against India at Delhi in December 1976, and after making 53, which was to prove his highest Test innings, took 7–46 and finished with match figures of 10–70?

7. Who has the best match figures by an England bowler against the West Indies, taking 8–86 and 5–70 at Port-of-Spain, Trinidad, in 1974 – Gary Sobers' final Test appearance – and a game that England won by 26 runs, so squaring the rubber?

8. Who bowled 316 eight-ball overs in five Test matches on his first tour of Australia in 1924–25, taking 38 wickets for 881 runs?

9. Who was the Kent left-arm medium-pace bowler who took 6 Australian wickets in each innings at The Oval on his Test début in 1890, recording match figures of 12–102, but made only one more Test match appearance, taking 2–39 against South Africa at Cape Town in March 1892?

10. Who was the Surrey medium-pace bowler who, between 1886 and 1896, took 112 Test wickets at an average of 10.75?

12 *Test match batting miscellany*

1. Which two players, at Madras in January 1985, became the first English batsmen to score double centuries in the same Test match innings?

2. Which New Zealand batsman, when scoring 158* against Pakistan in January 1985, passed 1,000 Test runs in only his twentieth Test match innings?

3. Which current player, during a twenty-five-day period in October and November 1975, scored a record 504 runs in his first five Test match innings?

4. Who scored 1,379 Test runs in 1974, a record for an English batsman in a calendar year?

5. Which opening batsman became the first Englishman to score a century in each innings of a Test match, scoring 140 and 111 against South Africa at Durban in February 1923, in what was to be his final Test match?

6. Which future Australian captain reached a century against England, at Sydney in March 1898 in ninety-one minutes, the fastest by an Australian in an Ashes Test, his 160 making him the first batsman to score three centuries and the first to exceed 500 runs in a Test series?

7. Who took 600 minutes to score 172 against England at Trent Bridge in July 1985, the second longest innings by an Australian batsman in England?

8. Who is the only Australian batsman, other than Don Bradman, to score 500 runs in a Test series in England on more than one occasion?

9. Who scored his second double century for Pakistan when sharing a third wicket stand of 397 with Javed Miandad, against Sri Lanka in October 1985?

10. Who was the future Australian opening batsman, batting down at number seven in only his fourth Test, who scored 134 – his maiden Test century – against South Africa at Cape Town in January 1967, the last Test century to be scored against the South Africans?

13 *Transfer trail*

1. Which Yorkshire-born bowler, who took 305 wickets in a 134-match career for Northamptonshire between 1980 and 1986, transferred his allegiance to Somerset in 1987, taking a Benson and Hedges Cup hat-trick for his new county v. the Combined Universities?

2. Which international cricketer, who had last played county cricket in 1984, joined Northamptonshire in 1987 as their second overseas player to Roger Harper?

3. Which Glasgow-born batsman, raised in South Africa, scored a century (on his first class début for Northamptonshire in 1985, but was released by the county at the end of the following season and joined Warwickshire?

4. Which current first-class umpire joined Glamorgan in 1980, his fourth county in a career that began with Sussex in 1966?

5. Which England Test player returned to his former county in 1987, after an interval of four years?

6. Which England bowler changed counties in 1986 and bowled 870 overs for his new team during the season, more than anyone else in first-class cricket?

7. Which cricketing veteran switched counties in 1983, having spent twenty-three years with his original team?

8. Who made his début for the county of his birth in 1984, twenty-two years after his first appearance in county cricket?

9. Which former Cambridge University Blue played for three different counties between 1968 and 1984?

10. Which legendary English bowler played four matches for Warwickshire between 1894 and 1896, and forty-six for Lancashire between 1899 and 1903, but for most of his long career turned his back on first-class county cricket, preferring to play for Staffordshire?

14 *One-day internationals*

1. Who, in March 1987 in his eighty-sixth innings, became the first player to exceed 2,500 runs in one-day internationals without scoring a century?

2. Who won a £15,000 car in February 1987 when, following his performances in the ashes series and the one-day Test matches in Australia, he was voted International Cricketer of the Year?

3. Which batsman scored two successive Perth Challenge centuries in January 1987 for Australia, v. England and Pakistan?

4. Which Australian bowler was hit for 18 runs off the first five balls of his final over, having conceded only 26 runs in his previous nine, when England gained an unlikely three-wicket victory in the World Series Cup match at Sydney in January 1987?

5. Off which Australian bowler did Ian Botham hit 26 in one over in his innings of 68 in the course of the Perth Challenge in January 1987?

6. In the absence of Mike Gatting, out with an injured toe, who captained England at Trent Bridge in the second Texaco Trophy match against Pakistan in May 1987?

7. Which batsman, coming in at number ten, scored 33 off twenty-two balls to win the third and deciding Texaco Trophy match for England against Pakistan by one wicket at Edgbaston in May 1987?

8. Who in January 1983 became the first Englishman to exceed 150 in a one-day international, when scoring 158 against New Zealand in a Benson and Hedges World Series Cup match in Brisbane?

9. Who in June 1985 became the first player to score 1,000 runs and take 100 wickets in one-day international cricket?

10. Which bowler, when taking 5–20 against New Zealand at Wellington in February 1984, achieved the best analysis by an Englishman in one-day internationals?

15 *Family connections*

1. Which pair of brothers scored Britannic Assurance double centuries within the space of a fortnight in the 1987 season?

2. Which father and son both scored centuries in the same innings against Warwickshire in July 1931, the fifty-two-year-old father making 183, and the son 100* when the match ended?

3. Who were the four cricketers involved in June 1922 when a father and son, batting together for Warwickshire, faced a father and son bowling for Derbyshire?

4. Who made his sole Test appearance for Australia against England at Adelaide in 1946–47, exactly a year before his youngest brother began a Test-match career that was to make him Australia's most dominant batsman for a decade?

5. Who was the first cricketer to play in more than fifty Test matches, with fifty-eight appearances for Australia between 1890 and 1912, following his father who played in the first ever Test match, and his uncle who captained Australia in the first three Tests that were played?

6. Who were the two brothers who opened the innings for South Africa and England respectively at Cape Town in March 1892, when a third brother and a cousin also played for England?

7. Who was dismissed by his cousin when New Zealand met Australia at Wellington in February 1986?

8. Which cricketing family established a record in 1986, when a third generation represented England?

9. Who are the New Zealand brothers, of whom the younger toured England as an eighteen-year-old in 1978, and dismissed Graham Gooch with his third ball in Test cricket, and the elder toured in 1983 and 1986, when he scored his maiden Test hundred at Trent Bridge to help his country to a second victory in England in fifty-five years?

10. Who were the father and son who captained England on all their Test match appearances?

16 *England v. India*

1. Which bowler in 1972–73 beat Vinoo Mankad's twenty-one-year-old record of 34 wickets in a series for India v. England, taking 35 at an average of 18.91?

2. Two men were flown out to join the 1963–64 MCC touring party in India in time for the Third Test – Colin Cowdrey, who scored two centuries in the remaining Tests, and which Middlesex batsman who scored one?

3. Who averaged 99 for England in the 1961–62 series in India when his 594 runs was an England record for a series against India which still stands?

4. Which bowler, in the 1952 Old Trafford Test, had an innings analysis of 8–31, equalling that of Australia's Frank Laver on the same ground forty-three years earlier?

5. Which bowler, in 1976–77, equalled the English record of 29 Indian wickets in a series, set by the above bowler in 1952?

6. Who scored a career-best 88* in front of his own crowd when sharing an eighth-wicket partnership of 168 with Ray Illingworth in 1971, which still ranks as an eighth-wicket record in England v. India Tests?

7. Who scored 125, his only Test century, for England against India at Kanpur in January 1973, the first Test century scored by an England player since Brian Luckhurst's, also against India, eighteen months earlier?

8. Which 20-year-old Indian batsman, playing in his third Test match, scored 133, at Headingley in 1952, his maiden first-class century, sharing a partnership of 222 with Vijay Hezare, an Indian record for the fourth wicket in Test cricket?

9. Which player, when scoring his second and last Test century, took nine hours for his 137* at Delhi in November 1951, becoming the first England player to bat throughout a whole day's play in a Test in India?

10. Which player, in the 1984–85 series, became the first batsman in Test cricket to score a century in each of his first three Test matches?

17 *Derbyshire*

1. Who in 1982 established a county record by scoring eight centuries in a season for Derbyshire, in twenty-one matches, totalling 1,941 runs from 30 completed innings at an average of 64.70?

2. Who scored seven centuries for Derbyshire in 1982, aggregating 1,830 runs at an average of 55.45?

3. Who was the former South African Test all-rounder who captained Derbyshire between 1976 and 1978?

4. Who was the twenty-two-year-old who scored 1,654 runs for Derbyshire, including four centuries, during the 1986 first-class season?

5. Which two Derbyshire batsmen, in a first round NatWest Trophy game against Cornwall in June 1986, shared in a record limited-overs partnership of 286, surpassing the previous record, 285 unbroken, set by Hampshire's Gordon Greenidge and David Turner in 1973?

6. Who preceded Bob Taylor as Derbyshire's wicketkeeper, making 394 appearances between 1947 and 1961 during which period he held 770 catches and took 105 stumpings?

7. Who was the Derbyshire fast-medium bowler who took 1,536 wickets for the county between 1939 and 1958, at an average of 17.67, and played in eight Test matches for England between 1947 and 1949?

8. Who was the Derbyshire pace bowler who took 1,670 wickets for the county between 1947 and 1963, at an average of 17.11, but played just twice for England, once in 1949 against New Zealand, and subsequently in 1961, at forty years of age, against Australia?

9. In which year, and captained by whom, did Derbyshire win the County Championship for the one and only time?

10. Which bowler, who made his England début in the 1932–33 'Bodyline' series against Australia, took a county record 168 wickets in a season in 1935, the year in which he was the last Derbyshire bowler to take all 10 wickets in an innings, finishing with 10–64 against Leicestershire?

18 Test match captains – England and Australia

1. Who were the opposing captains in the Centenary Test at Melbourne in March 1977?

2. Who captained England in the Centenary Test at Lord's in August and September 1980?

3. Who was the last England captain to lose an Ashes series?

4. Which two players were Test match captains for the one and only time, at Headingley in July 1968, both Colin Cowdrey and Bill Lawry being injured?

5. Who in June 1961 captained Australia for the only time, at Lord's, this being his seventy-first Test match?

6. Who was the Australian captain on the 1956 tour of England, when Jim Laker's haul of 19 wickets at Old Trafford secured the Ashes for the home side?

7. Who was the Australian captain in the so-called 'Bodyline' series of 1932–33?

8. Which Australian captained his country in ten Test matches, all against England, and achieved the best pro-rata record of any captain in the series, recording eight wins and two draws?

9. Who were the respective captains in the 1905 Ashes Test series in England who, by a remarkable coincidence, were born on the same day?

10. Who were the respective captains in March 1877 when the first official Test match was played in Melbourne?

19 *Prowess in other sports*

1. Which opening batsman made his Test début for New Zealand against the West Indies at Christchurch in March 1987, having represented his country at badminton in the 1986 Commonwealth Games at Edinburgh?

2. Which future England cricket international and current county captain scored one of Cambridge's three tries in the 1978 Varsity Rugby Match?

3. Which left-handed bat and fine field, capped three times by England in 1976 and 1977, has also played rugby for the England Under-23 team?

4. Who opened the batting for England v. New Zealand at Lord's in June 1931, his only Test match, and played outside-left for England against Scotland in 1933, his only football international?

5. Who at twenty years of age played in five Tests for South Africa v. England in 1929, scoring 129 at Headingley, batting at number seven, and subsequently played full-back for England in ten Rugby Union internationals between 1934 and 1937?

6. Those legendary South Africans Eddie Barlow, Colin Bland and Peter Pollock all made their Test débuts against New Zealand at Durban in December 1961. Which other player, winning the first of his three caps for South Africa, had previously represented Scotland eight times as a Rugby centre three-quarter in 1954 and 1955?

7. Which amateur played seventy-one matches for Hampshire between 1878 and 1908, three times for England between 1896 and 1906, having in 1881 won an FA Cup winners' medal when scoring the first goal in Old Carthusians' 3–0 victory over Old Etonians?

8. Who toured England in 1947–48 with the Australian Rugby League team, and South Africa in 1949–50 with the Australian cricket team, before playing five seasons with Nottinghamshire, for which county he took four wickets in four balls against Leicestershire in the 1956 Championship?

9. Which England hockey captain led Surrey to win the County Cricket Championship in 1914, and in 1920 was a member of the Great Britain hockey team which won an Olympic gold medal at the Olympic Games?

10. Which Old Harrovian played nine matches for Yorkshire in 1911 and 1912, and in 1925 rode Double Chance to win the Grand National at Aintree?

20 Touring sides against the Counties

1. Who scored 211* for Pakistan against Sussex in May 1987, just three days after his late arrival in England?

2. Who also scored 211* for Pakistan against Sussex, this time in 1982, sharing an opening stand of 319 with Mohsin Khan?

3. Who scored 201* for the West Indies against Glamorgan in 1969, and again in 1976, when he equalled a seventy-three-year-old world record by reaching his double century in only 120 minutes?

4. Who scored 147*, including 13 sixes, against Glamorgan in 1967, his eighty-nine-minute innings presumably having some say in his being taken on to the Welsh county's staff in 1968?

5. Which touring bowler headed the 1963 first-class averages, taking 119 wickets at 12.82, including 32 wickets at 16.21 in the Test series?

6. Which two Australian tourists headed the 1961 first-class batting averages, the only two players to have averages in excess of 60 for the season?

7. Who was the South African who topped the first-class batting averages in England in 1955, scoring 1,871 runs at 58.46, including 476 in the Test matches at 52.88?

8. Which South African bowler took 143 wickets at 15.75, in the 1955 English season, his record in the Test series being 26 at 21.84?

9. Which Australian batsman made a career-best 290 against Gloucestershire at Bristol in 1948, one of seven centuries he scored on the tour?

10. Which Australian bowler took 102 wickets on the 1948 tour of England, which was exactly the same as the number of runs he was to score on the 1953 tour?

21 Essex

1. Which batsman, in the 1985 County Championship, scored 1,368 runs for Essex including six centuries, his seventeen innings leaving him with an average of 91.20 for the season in Championship matches alone?

2. Who took 100 wickets for Essex in the 1986 County Championship, the first time that he has achieved the feat?

3. Which Essex player celebrated his twenty-sixth birthday on 27 July 1985 by equalling a world record in the County Championship match against Somerset at Taunton?

4. In which year did Essex win the County Championship for the first time?

5. Which player, between 1946 and 1967, scored 21,460 runs and took 1,593 wickets for Essex, captaining the side from 1961 to 1966?

6. Who in 1965 was the last Essex player to achieve the 'double' of 1,000 runs and 100 wickets in a season, finishing with 1,172 runs from his fifty-five innings and taking 125 wickets in total?

7. Who scored 2,051 runs for Essex, including eight centuries, in the 1983 County Championship, the first batsman to hit 2,000 runs in a season for the county since Doug Insole in 1955?

8. Who was the South African who played fifty-four matches for Essex in 1968 and 1969, scoring 2,674 runs at an average of 34.72, and in March 1970 scored South Africa's last century in official Test matches?

9. Which former England captain led Essex from 1911 to 1928 and, during a career which began in 1901, scored 17,915 runs and took 1,443 wickets for the county?

10. Who in 1904 scored 343* against Derbyshire at Chesterfield, a record for an individual innings for the county which still stands, and an innings containing a world record of sixty-eight boundary hits?

22 One-day cricket – The Sunday League

1. Which future Test player scored the first ever century in the John Player League in 1969, in a game that received live coverage on BBC Television?

2. Which county won the inaugural John Player League championship in 1969, retained it in 1970, but have never since won the title?

3. Who took 7 wickets for 15 runs for Yorkshire against Worcestershire at Headingley in 1969, the best analysis in the competition by an Englishman?

4. Which England international, playing for Derbyshire against Sussex at Derby in 1970, achieved the unprecedented feat of taking 4 wickets in four balls in the competition?

5. Which county captain, had the remarkable bowling analysis of eight overs, all maidens, in a John Player League match against Essex in 1969?

6. Which county, playing against Derbyshire, scored 307 runs off only 38 overs in 1975, the first time that an innings of 300 was registered in the John Player League?

7. Which county was bowled out for just 23 runs in under twenty overs by Yorkshire at Headingley in 1974?

8. Who was the first batsman to score 6,000 runs in the John Player League, reaching this target in 1982, his final season in first-class cricket?

9. Who was the first batsman to score 7,000 runs in the Sunday League, reaching the target in 1987, his final season in first-class cricket, having scored a record 6,861 runs in the John Player League alone?

10. Which county would have won the 1976 John Player League championship, had they avoided defeat in their final game against Glamorgan at Cardiff, but the home side secured a run-out off the last ball of the match, to win by one run?

23 *Career statistics – Wicket-keepers*

1. Which wicket-keeper in 1976 surpassed both Herbert Strudwick's career records of 1,242 catches and 1,496 total dismissals?

2. Which Leicestershire-born wicket-keeper, who played for his home county from 1937 to 1939 before moving on to Derbyshire after the war, retired in 1961 with a career record of 11,411 runs and 1,043 dismissals?

3. Which player, seventeen years after his début as an eighteen-year-old schoolboy, became the twenty-second wicket-keeper in history to record 1,000 career dismissals, and the first to do so since Roger Tolchard in 1983, when catching Lancashire's David Varey in June 1987?

4. Which current Test match umpire achieved 827 wicket-keeping dismissals for Gloucestershire in 406 matches between 1957 and 1971?

5. Who was the player who, succeeding his brother as Yorkshire's wicket-keeper, claimed 1,327 dismissals between 1888 and 1909, becoming the first of the twenty-two to date to exceed 1,000?

6. Which Somerset wicket-keeper holds the post-war record for stumpings, with 332 out of 1,084 dismissals between 1948 and 1964?

7. Who registered a record 415 stumpings out of 1,113 dismissals between 1926 and 1951?

8. Who began the great tradition of Kent wicket-keepers, claiming 1,328 dismissals between 1895 and 1914, although unlike his successors he was never to play for England?

9. Who claimed 1,071 dismissals between 1955 and 1975, catching 96 in 1960, a first-class record for catches in a season?

10. Who has taken the most dismissals by an overseas wicket-keeper, recording 841 between 1960 and 1981 and overtaking Farokh Engineer's previous record of 824 between 1958 and 1976?

24 *Christian names*

Identify the following post-war England Test cricketers from their middle names and potted Test career records:

	Middle name	Number of Tests	Year of first Test	Year of last Test	Runs	Wickets	Catches
1.	Augustine	49	1965	1976	772	202	16
2.	Barker	66	1951	1961	4,537	–	42
3.	Billson	12†	1983	1987	134	47	5
4.	Dylan	90	1971	1984	840	325	39
5.	Henri	51†	1975	1987	875	125	42
6.	Knight	50	1958	1972	2,278	1	53
7.	Lyall	8†	1983	1986	392	3	5
8.	Orlando	3†	1981	1981	71	–	3
9.	Sewards	67	1952	1965	981	307	64
10.	Shackleton	1†	1984		12	2	–

† = Total up to and including June 1988

25 *Glamorgan*

1. Who was the nineteen-year-old, playing his first County Championship match, who reached 102 for Glamorgan, against Yorkshire at Swansea in August 1985 with a third successive six off Phil Carrick?

2. Who was the twenty-two-year-old who replaced Rodney Ontong as Glamorgan captain during the Championship match against Northamptonshire in July 1986?

3. Which Glamorgan batsman scored 36,049 runs between 1957 and 1983, the highest total in first-class cricket by a player who has never played in an official Test match?

4. Who captained Glamorgan from 1947 to 1960, leading the county to their first Championship in 1948?

5. Who was the left-handed all-rounder who played in fifteen Test matches for England between 1948 and 1952, a record number by a Glamorgan player, later equalled by Jeff Jones?

6. Who took 2,174 wickets for Glamorgan between 1950 and 1972, the highest number in first-class cricket by a player who was never selected for a Test match?

7. Which current broadcaster established himself as one of the great 'leg trap' fielders in cricket, holding 656 catches for Glamorgan in 437 matches between 1955 and 1972?

8. Who was the right-arm spin bowler who played for Glamorgan in 1921, their initial season in the County Championship, captained the county for the first time in 1924, and at the age of fifty was an important member of the Championship-winning team in 1948?

9. Which player, who had not appeared in county cricket since leaving Nottinghamshire in 1982, scored a Benson and Hedges century in May 1987 for the Minor Counties against Glamorgan, so impressing the county that he was taken onto the staff and, before the end of the season, scored 135 against Worcestershire and 90 against the touring Pakistanis?

10. Which two Glamorgan players both took their 500th first-class wickets during the 1984 season?

26 Test match grounds

1. Which Test match ground, besides Old Trafford, has suffered the ignominy of having a Test Match abandoned, because of rain, without a ball being bowled?

2. Which ground, now defunct in cricket terms, hosted its only Test match in July 1902?

3. On which ground was the infamous 'Timeless Test' played in March 1939, the game eventually remaining unfinished after eleven days' effort because the touring MCC team had to catch their boat home?

4. Which ground in September 1986 played host to the second ever tied Test in the history of Test match cricket?

5. In which Test match centre is the Basin Reserve ground, which staged its first Test in 1930?

6. At which venue, staging only its second Test match, did Sunil Gavaskar become the first player to reach 10,000 runs in Test cricket, a feat which he achieved in March 1987 in the home series against Pakistan?

7. In which two cities, one in South Africa and the other in India, has Test cricket been played at three separate venues?

8. In which city, apart from London, has there been a Test match venue known as Lord's?

9. Only two players have made centuries at Lord's on their Test match débuts: Henry Graham for Australia v. England in 1893, and who else, seventy-six years later?

10. Who in June 1939 became the only man to have scored a century in each innings of a Lord's Test match?

27 Test cricket – Not England

1. Who was the wicket-keeper who played in both Tests for the West Indies against New Zealand in February 1952, and four years later was making his début for New Zealand against the West Indies?

2. Who, when playing against Australia at Johannesburg in December 1935, scored 231, South Africa's highest individual score in Test cricket until Eric Rowan's 236 at Headingley in 1951, and in the process became the first player to score a duck and a double century in the same Test?

3. Two West Indians, both batsmen, made their Test débuts in the Brisbane tied Test in December 1960: Cammie Smith, who played in four further Tests, and which other player, who played once more in that series before making his only two other appearances when opening the batting in England in 1966?

4. Which Australian was run out in both innings of the Brisbane Tied Test in December 1960?

5. Which man made his South African début v. New Zealand in December 1961, in the same match as Eddie Barlow, Colin Bland and Peter Pollock? He was to take 28 wickets in the series at 18.29, his 8–53 at Johannesburg being an innings record in Tests between the two countries, but was never selected for his country thereafter.

6. Who, playing for Australia v. West Indies at Kingston, Jamaica, in April 1978, scored 122, his one and only Test century in fifteen Tests, becoming Vanburn Holder's 100th wicket in Tests, and followed it up with 97 in the second innings?

7. Who was the future captain of New Zealand who, at Auckland in March 1964, scored 138, the last century in a New Zealand v. South Africa Test match?

8. Which Australian opening batsman, who made his Test début at Brisbane in November 1954 in the same match as Colin Cowdrey, scored the only century of his nineteen-match Test career when batting all day for 101 in Madras in January 1960?

9. Who in October 1976 became the first batsman to score a century before lunch on the first morning of a Test match against opposition other than England?

10. Who scored his only century in his fifteen-Test career when he made 101 in 187 minutes in an Australian record seventh-wicket partnership of 217 with Doug Walters, against New Zealand in Christchurch in February 1977?

28 *England v. Australia – Test miscellany*

1. Who started his twelve-year Test career at Headingley in 1975 by taking 5 Australian first innings wickets for 28 runs, his 'victims' including the Chappell brothers, Ross Edwards (first ball) and Doug Walters?

2. Who was the near-veteran fast bowler who lost his England place after match figures of 0–111 in the First Test at Brisbane in 1974–75, but returned for the final Test at Melbourne and took nine wickets in the match, including 6–38 in the first innings?

3. Who in January 1975 captained England for the only time, when Mike Denness left himself out of the Fourth Test Match at Sydney, after scoring only 65 runs in six innings in the first three matches of the series?

4. Which England batsman was dismissed by Dennis Lillee without scoring in his last three innings in the 1974–75 Ashes series?

5. Who captured 16 England wickets for 137 at Lord's in 1972, at that time a record for a bowler making his début in Test cricket?

6. Which English bowler suffered a harsh introduction to Test match cricket when bowling seventy-seven overs in an innings on his début against Australia at Old Trafford in 1964, though his figures of 2–118 remained comparatively respectable?

7. Who spearheaded England's success in the 1970–71 Ashes series, taking 31 wickets at an average of 22.84?

8. Who had figures of 7–50 in Australia's second innings at The Oval in the 1968 series, so giving England a victory with five minutes to spare after a storm had held up play for three hours?

9. Who, in only his second Test match, batted 250 minutes to score 56 of Australia's total of 125 in the innings referred to above, being last out, leg before wicket padding up?

10. Who scored 554 runs for England in the 1968 series against Australia, at an average of 61.56, and 648 in 1970–71, at an average of 72.00?

29 *Gloucestershire*

1. Who scored 2,306 runs, including ten centuries, for Gloucestershire in 1981 at an average of 88.69?

2. Which Gloucestershire player has achieved the unique (to him) feat of twice performing the hat-trick by dismissing all three victims leg before wicket?

3. Which Gloucestershire player, playing against Nottinghamshire in 1966, equalled the record of 7 catches by a non-wicket-keeper in one innings of a first-class match?

4. Which Gloucestershire player, in the space of six days at Cheltenham in August 1928, held 10 catches in a match against Surrey, a world record for a non-wicket-keeper, scored a century in both innings of the same match and, in the following game against Worcestershire, took 15 wickets, including 9–23 in the first innings?

5. Who in 1964 was the last player to achieve the 'double' of 1,000 runs and 100 wickets in a season for Gloucestershire?

6. Who scored 30,218 runs and took 718 catches in 585 appearances for Gloucestershire between 1948 and 1974?

7. Which great bowler took 3,170 wickets for Gloucestershire, including six hat-tricks, in a record 602 appearances for the county between 1903 and 1935?

8. Which famous cricketer captained Gloucestershire from 1900 to 1912 and, in a county career of 345 games between 1894 and 1914, scored 18,936 runs, took 620 wickets and held 356 catches?

9. Who in 1986 became the youngest player to score a century for Gloucestershire in a Championship game, recording 116* against Sussex, at the age of 18 years and 54 days?

10. Who was Gloucestershire's opening batsman who in May 1948, two months before his only Test appearance, carried his bat for 104* out of a total of 156 in the county's match against Oxford University?

30 One-day internationals

1. Who scored 119 and took 5–41 in a one-day international at Dunedin in March 1987, the first time that anyone had achieved such an all-round performance in any one match in this form of international cricket?

2. Who scored eighteen runs off the first five balls of the final over to gain England victory over Australia in a World Series Cup match at Sydney in January 1987?

3. Which England bowler took most wickets in addition to conceding the lowest run-rate per over in the 1987 World Series Cup in Australia?

4. Who were the opening pair who in September 1986 in Jaipur, India, both scored centuries in a partnership of 212, but found themselves on the losing side?

5. Who in Sharjah in April 1986 helped to win the inaugural Five-Nation Australasia Cup for his country, his innings of 116* being climaxed by a six off the last ball of the match?

6. Who scored 142* for England against New Zealand at Old Trafford in July 1986, only his third one-day international and his first for six years?

7. Who scored England's only century on the 1985–86 tour of the West Indies with 129*, scored off only thirty-seven overs, in the second one-day international, at Port-of-Spain, Trinidad?

8. Which West Indian bowler conceded 62 runs from his nine overs in the above game, in stark contrast to his figures in the three other one-day matches in the series, in which he bowled twenty-five overs for just 46 runs?

9. Who scored three unbeaten centuries for the West Indies in four one-day internationals against Australia in February and April 1984?

10. Who scored three successive centuries for Pakistan against India in One-day internationals in December 1982 and January 1983?

31 *University cricket*

1. Who, playing against Derbyshire in May 1987, became the first Cambridge undergraduate to carry his bat through a completed innings since Charles Ponniah against Leicestershire in 1967?

2. Which player in 1987 became only the third Oxford University freshman to score a century in the Varsity match at Lord's, following in the illustrious footsteps of Mike Smith (1954) and the Nawab of Pataudi (1960)?

3. Who was the freshman who scored 174 for Cambridge in the 1986 Varsity match, the seventh highest innings in the 142-year history of the fixture?

4. Who scored a career-best 149 for Oxford in the 1985 Varsity match, and returned his best ever bowling figures with 8–52 in Cambridge's first innings?

5. Who scored a century for Cambridge in both innings of the 1983 Varsity match, the first time this feat had been achieved in the fixture?

6. Who was the Cambridge freshman and future England batsman who scored the first double century of the 1976 season, an innings of 215 against Essex on the last day of April?

7. Who scored a century for Oxford in three consecutive Varsity matches between 1954 and 1956?

8. Who was the Oxford University captain who scored a century in both innings of the 1961 match against Yorkshire, only the tenth player ever to achieve this feat?

9. Who were the two Cambridge University under-graduates who, against Essex in 1949, scored undefeated double centuries in a then English record second-wicket partnership of 429?

10. Which two future Test players made century opening partnerships for Cambridge University in both innings of the 1960 match against Somerset at Taunton when, uniquely, Graham Atkinson and Roy Virgin performed the same feat for the home side?

32 *Australian cricket*

1. Which Australian state in 1926 scored 1,107, the highest innings total in first-class cricket?

2. Who scored 452* for New South Wales against Queensland in January 1930, the highest score in Australian first-class cricket?

3. Who scored 429 for Victoria against Tasmania in 1922–23 and 437 against Queensland in 1927–28, the only instance in first-class cricket of a batsman exceeding 400 runs on more than one occasion?

4. Who were the two batsmen who set a world record when adding 307 for the last wicket for New South Wales against Victoria on Christmas Day and Boxing Day 1928, taking the score from 113–9 to 420?

5. Who in 1983–84 surpassed Don Bradman's record of 8,896 runs in Sheffield Shield matches?

6. Which English bowler took a record 302 wickets for Western Australia, a total that has subsequently been surpassed only by Dennis Lillee?

7. Which great all-round cricketer has twice performed the 'double' of 1,000 runs and 50 wickets in a Sheffield Shield season, a feat that no one else has performed even once?

8. Who in February 1977 became the first Australian to score a century in each innings of two successive first-class matches, scoring 185 and 105 against Queensland and 135 and 156 against New South Wales, both games being played on his home ground in Adelaide?

9. Who scored a record 262 for Western Australia against Victoria at Perth in the 1986–87 Sheffield Shield Final, helping his state to their highest ever innings total of 654?

10. Which English batsman scored 243 for Western Australia at Brisbane in 1968, the highest individual innings for the state until the 1986–87 Sheffield Shield Final?

33 *Hampshire*

1. Who established a new record for Hampshire in 1986, scoring four hundreds in successive innings?

2. Who, in 204 matches between 1968 and 1978, scored 15,607 runs for Hampshire, at an average of 50.50?

3. Who took 100 wickets in a season for Hampshire on two occasions, the first in 1955 and the second in 1971?

4. Who captured 2,669 wickets for Hampshire in 583 matches between 1948 and 1969, the only post-war player to record more than 2,500 dismissals in county cricket?

5. Which Hampshire batsman, between 1905 and 1936, scored 48,892 runs for the county, a record for any individual in county cricket alone?

6. Who was the aristocrat who captained Hampshire from 1919 to 1933, as well as leading England in three Tests in 1921?

7. Who took 119 wickets for Hampshire in 1974, his first Championship season for the county, at an average of 13.62?

8. Who in 1961 captained the Hampshire side that won the County Championship for the first time?

9. Who in his twenty-second season with the county scored a career-best 184* for Hampshire against Gloucestershire in July 1987?

10. Who has shared in both the county's two best opening partnerships – 347 against Warwickshire in 1987 and 250 against Northamptonshire in 1986?

34 *Test match batting miscellany*

1. Who scored 268 for Australia against Pakistan in December 1983, a score only bettered in Test cricket by Don Bradman, Bobby Simpson and Bob Cowper amongst Australians?

2. Who scored 68, his highest first-class innings, when sharing in a West Indies record ninth-wicket stand of 161 with Clive Lloyd in Calcutta in December 1983?

3. Who in March 1969 ended his Test career with a flourish by hitting 258, a record for a final Test innings, when playing against New Zealand in Christchurch, ending the three-match series with an average of 111.60?

4. Which England batsman, in December 1984 in Bombay, made his first Test century in his fifty-fourth innings, having scored 1,144 runs at 23.83 in his thirty previous Test matches?

5. Which West Indian fast bowler, playing in his only Test in the series, scored a career-best 77 against England at Old Trafford in July 1984, sharing a sixth-wicket partnership of 170 with Gordon Greenidge?

6. Who was the nineteen-year-old New Zealand left-hander who toured South Africa in 1953–54 without having played in a first-class match, and in his second Test, in Cape Town, was run out for 99 and was never to make a Test century?

7. Who in 1929 became the first batsman to score four centuries in a Test series in England, climaxing the series against South Africa with a hundred in each innings at The Oval?

8. Who was the Indian batsman who scored 2,084 runs in forty Test matches between 1969 and 1981, a record number for a player who failed to reach a century, his highest score among his 16 fifties being 97?

9. Who, playing for Pakistan against India at Faisalabad in October 1984, became the first batsman to be dismissed for 199 in Test cricket?

10. Who, at Sydney in December 1984, scored 173 for Australia, ten more than the West Indies first innings total, as the West Indians were beaten for the first time in twenty-seven Tests, by an innings and 55 runs?

35 Hundreds

1. Who, in spite of scoring four Test centuries in the 1984 English first-class season, only scored one in the County Championship, at Worcester in September, which at 83 minutes was the fastest of the season until Mike Gatting upstaged it later in the same afternoon?

2. Which Sussex batsman, who was to retire in 1955 with 34,380 first-class runs, a record then for a player who had not appeared in Test cricket, scored twelve centuries for the county in 1949 at the age of thirty-nine?

3. Which two young players, both to be capped by their counties later in the month, scored centuries before lunch on the 1 August 1987?

4. Who scored 100* on his first-class début, against Nottinghamshire in September 1978, and in August 1987, after a further 100-odd County Championship innings for his only county, scored the second century of his Championship career, 102 against Middlesex?

5. Who scored eighteen centuries in one season, a record which will almost certainly never be surpassed while the reduced Championship programme is in operation?

6. Who scored ninety-one first-class centuries between his fortieth and fiftieth birthdays?

7. Who is the only English batsman to score six hundreds in consecutive innings?

8. Who scored seventy-six centuries in a career which extended from 1928 to 1955, by far the highest number by a player who never appeared in a Test match?

9. Who were the five Australian batsmen who scored centuries against the West Indies at Sabina Park, Kingston, in June 1955, when Australia registered their record innings total of 758–8 declared?

10. Who scored a century for the West Indies in each innings of this same match, achieving two records that have never been equalled: five centuries in one Test series, and a century in both innings of a Test on two occasions in the same series?

36 West Indies batsmen

1. Who became the only post-war batsman to be dismissed for 99 on his Test début, when being trapped leg before by England's acting captain, Ken Cranston, at Bridgetown in January 1948?

2. Who scored 4,399 runs in sixty-six Test appearances between 1972 and 1980, the most Test runs by a West Indian who has not scored a Test double century?

3. Which West Indies batsman, in scoring the third Test double century of his career in March 1987, became the first player to score a Test double century in New Zealand since Doug Walters in February 1977?

4. Which West Indian batsman has the distinction of being the only player to feature in two partnerships in excess of 500 runs, scoring a career-best 308* when adding 502 with John Goddard for Barbados against Trinidad in 1943–44, a world record for the fourth wicket which was surpassed two years later when he contributed 255* to a stand of 574 with Clyde Walcott, also against Trinidad?

5. Which West Indian is the only batsman to score centuries in five consecutive Test Match innings, the remarkable sequence ending when he was run out for 90 in the sixth?

6. Who scored the only Test match triple century by a West Indian against England, making 302 out of 551 at Bridgetown, Barbados, in March 1974?

7. Who was the first West Indian to make a Test match century and subsequently a double century, achieving both against England in January and February 1930, scoring 122 at Bridgetown in the first ever Test match in the Caribbean, and 209 at Georgetown?

8. Who became the first batsman to score four Test hundreds before the age of twenty-one when, in the above series, he scored 176 at Bridgetown, 114 and 112 at Georgetown and 223 at Kingston, totalling 703 runs in four Test matches, at an average of 87.87?

9. Who scored his maiden Test century and the highest innings of his career when amassing 256 against India at Calcutta, to celebrate the New Year in 1958–59, subsequently scoring fourteen more hundreds as he compiled over 6,000 runs in Test cricket?

10. When Gary Sobers made his world best 365* against Pakistan at Sabina Park, Kingston, in 1958, who partnered him in a second-wicket stand of 446, before being run out for 260, his highest Test score?

37 Kent

1. Who, at Folkestone in September 1986, took 7 Warwickshire wickets for eleven runs in 35 overs and 5 balls which included 29 maidens?

2. Who took 98 Championship wickets for Kent during the 1986 season?

3. Which Kent bowler in 1985 became the first Englishman for seven years to lead the first-class bowling averages, taking 65 wickets at an average of 17.20, a tally considerably augmented by 17 wickets at an average of 10.88 in two Test matches against Australia?

4. Who, in 412 Championship games for Kent between 1950 and 1975, scored 23,779 runs at an average of 42, took 27 wickets and held 405 catches?

5. Which Kent batsman holds the unique record of scoring a double century in both innings of a first-class match, hitting 244 and 202* against Essex in 1938?

6. Which opening batsman scored a triple century on two occasions, the only Kent player to compile an innings of 300 runs in a Championship game, and also has the distinction of being the only active player in first-class cricket both before the First World War and after the Second?

7. Who was the only Kent bowler to take more than 200 Championship wickets in a season, performing the feat seven times in eight seasons between 1928 and 1935?

8. Which Kent and England slow left-arm bowler had match figures of 17–48 against Northamptonshire in 1907, still the best performance by any bowler in a Championship match?

9. Who, in 186 matches for Kent between 1964 and 1977, scored only 404 runs, in contrast to taking 614 wickets?

10. Who scored a career-best 221* for Kent against the touring Sri Lankans in August 1984?

38 England v. Australia – Test miscellany

1. Who, when scoring 120 at Lord's in 1934, became the first wicket-keeper to score a century in an Ashes Test match?

2. Who captained Australia against England in sixteen Test matches and subsequently played once for England, against South Africa?

3. Who, in forty-one Test matches, scored a record 3,636 runs for England against Australia?

4. Who, in the course of an eleven-year Test career, scored 2,741 runs for England against Australia in just twenty-seven matches at an average of 66.85?

5. Which gifted left-handed batsman of the 'Golden Age' was the first player from either side to score over 2,000 runs in England v. Australia Test matches, finishing up with a total aggregate of 2,660?

6. Who has both bowled most balls and taken most wickets in England v. Australia Test matches?

7. Which England all-rounder had a highest score against Australia of 179 at Melbourne in 1911–12 and a best innings bowling performance of 8–68, also at Melbourne, in January 1904?

8. Who was the twenty-one-year-old spin bowler who took 6–79 in Australia's second innings at Old Trafford in the First Test of the 1968 series, but in a twenty-five-match Test career, spread over three decades, was never again to play against Australia?

9. Which pair bowled unchanged for England at Brisbane in December 1936, when Australia were dismissed in their second innings in just twelve overs and three balls, for a total of 58?

10. Which Australian batsman was dismissed for 99 at Trent Bridge in 1934, in his maiden Test innings, caught at the wicket off the bowling of another player making his Test début, Ken Farnes?

39 *England v. New Zealand*

1. Which New Zealander, in the course of the 1986 series against England, became in the First Test Phil Edmonds's 100th Test wicket, and in the Third, Ian Botham's 356th, putting him above Dennis Lillee in the all-time list?

2. Whose record of 20 wickets in a series for New Zealand v. England, set in 1958, did Richard Hadlee surpass in 1983, when bowling Norman Cowans at Trent Bridge?

3. Who, in the course of taking 7–143 at Wellington in January 1984, the best innings analysis for New Zealand in a home Test against England, dismissed Allan Lamb to become the fifth New Zealand bowler to reach 100 Test wickets?

4. Who scored 99 for New Zealand at Christchurch in February 1984, and finished with match figures of 8–44 when England scored 82 and 93, bowled out for under 100 in both innings of a Test for the first time this century?

5. Who was left out of the 1965 Lord's Test against New Zealand for taking 437 minutes to compile his 137 in the previous match at Edgbaston, but returned to the fold at Headingley, contributing 163 out of a 369–run second-wicket partnership with John Edrich, thus ending the series with exactly 300 runs in two innings?

6. Which two New Zealanders at Trent Bridge in 1973 scored 176 and 116 respectively, the latter's being a maiden Test century, as New Zealand made 440 in their second innings, falling just 39 runs short of their victory target?

7. Who were the respective captains at Wellington in February 1978 when New Zealand beat England by 72 runs to register their first victory in the forty-eight Tests between the two countries?

8. Although Richard Hadlee was the New Zealand hero in the above match, taking 6 for 2 as England were routed for 64 in their second innings, and ten wickets in the match, who gave him admirable support with three 'victims' in each innings, not only reaching 100 wickets in Tests but twice dismissing Geoff Boycott?

9. Who scored 206 for New Zealand at Lord's in 1949, which remains the only double century for the 'Kiwis' against England?

10. When New Zealand were dismissed for a record low Test match innings of 26 at Eden Park, Auckland, in March 1955, which England bowler took 3 second innings wickets in four balls, having also been on a hat-trick in the first innings?

40 *The Prudential World Cup*

1. Which New Zealand bowler conceded a record 105 runs from his twelve overs in the opening game of the 1983 Prudential World Cup against England?

2. Which team scored 338 against Sri Lanka in the 1983 Prudential World Cup, the highest score to date in the competition?

3. Kim Hughes led Australia in their first five group matches in the 1983 World Cup but, when injured, was replaced as captain for the last match by which player, who has never since led his country in Test cricket?

4. Which country, at Old Trafford in 1983, handed the West Indies their first defeat in a Prudential World Cup match?

5. Who took a competition record 7 wickets for 51 runs as the West Indies dismissed Australia for 151 in thirty-one overs at Headingley in 1983?

6. Who scored only the second century by an Australian in three Prudential World Cup tournaments when registering 110 against India at Nottingham in 1983?

7. Who played arguably the greatest of all one-day innings when, coming in at 17–5, he scored 175* in 181 minutes, taking his team to 266–8 against Zimbabwe in their 1983 Prudential World Cup encounter at Tunbridge Wells?

8. Who won the Man of the Match award for India in both the 1983 Prudential World Cup semi-final and final, taking, in the latter, 3 wickets for 12 runs after scoring 26 of his country's innings of 183?

9. Who was the Zimbabwe captain who, against Australia in the 1983 Prudential World Cup, became the first player to score a fifty and take 4 wickets in the same World Cup match?

10. Who kept wicket for England in their seven games in the 1983 Prudential World Cup tournament, but has not yet been selected to play in a Test match?

41 *Lancashire*

1. Who returned to first team cricket in 1987, leading Lancashire to second place in the County Championship, having captained their Second XI the previous season?

2. Which Lancashire player, scoring 128 at Old Trafford and 147 at Headingley in 1985, became the first since Barry Wood in 1970 to score centuries in both the seasonal 'Roses' matches?

3. Who in 1965 totalled 2,037 runs for Lancashire without scoring a century, his highest score being 85 v. Warwickshire at Blackpool?

4. Who was the Australian-born football league goalkeeper, most notably with Bolton Wanderers, who held 555 catches for Lancashire in 452 Championship appearances between 1949 and 1964?

5. Who started the 1987 first-class season as Lancashire's third choice wicket-keeper, but in July, in his fourth first-class match, turned batsman and scored 130 against Northamptonshire, his maiden first-class century, after having come in as night-watchman?

6. Who was the great Australian fast bowler who took 1,053 wickets for Lancashire in 217 matches between 1924 and 1931?

7. Who was the Lancashire and later England captain who scored a Championship record 424 runs in an innings, against Somerset in 1895, the only time that an individual score of 400 has been recorded in this country, prior to 1988?

8. Who took 101 Championship wickets in 1973, and 112 in 1975, the only Lancashire bowler to have recorded one hundred wickets in a season since the Championship programme was reduced in 1969?

9. Who captained Lancashire from 1926 to 1928, taking the county to the Championship in each of the three seasons?

10. Who was the twenty-four-year-old slow left-arm bowler who had match figures of 12 wickets for 57 runs against Warwickshire in July 1987, including a career-best 7 for 15 from his twenty-one overs in the first innings?

42 England batsmen

1. Who averaged more than 30 runs per innings more than any other England batsman in the controversial three-match series v. Pakistan in 1987–88?

2. Which batsman was dropped by England after the Lord's Test against the 1980 West Indians, to be recalled virtually twelve months to the day later, against Australia at Trent Bridge? However, going in first wicket down, he was unlucky enough to be dismissed for a pair.

3. Which batsman, on successive tours of Australia and New Zealand, is the only Englishman to twice score two double centuries in a single Test series, on both occasions in successive innings?

4. Which thirty-nine-year-old scored a career-best 325 in his final Test match?

5. Which English batsman scored twenty-two Test centuries but never reached 200, his highest score being 182 against Pakistan at The Oval in 1962?

6. Which batsman, still actively involved in Test cricket, never scored a Test century, his highest score being 87 in the First Test against the West Indies at Old Trafford in June 1963, which turned out to be the highest score of the series by an Englishman?

7. When Chris Broad and Tim Robinson opened the batting for England against Pakistan at Lord's in 1987 they were the first pair from the same county to open for England for almost twenty years to the day, when which pair, in June 1967, also opened at Lord's, in the Second Test against India?

8. Who was the only England batsman to score a double century against both Australia and South Africa?

9. Which England player scored 1,000 Test runs in a calendar year in 1961, only the second after Denis Compton to do so, and repeated the feat two years later in 1963?

10. Which man, in the 1947 Test series against South Africa, became only the second Englishman after Herbert Sutcliffe eighteen years earlier, also against South Africa, to score four Test centuries in an English summer?

43 *Career statistics – Bowlers*

1. Which Barbados-born fast-medium bowler, who took 234 wickets in a county career with Warwickshire between 1962 and 1966, had originally sprung to prominence in 1961, when he took a wicket with his first ball in each innings of his first-class début for Scotland against MCC, while studying medicine at Edinburgh University?

2. Who, in a career foreshortened by health problems, took 708 wickets at the exceptional average of 15.44, the highlight being 1951, his first full season, when as an unknown he claimed 200 wickets at 14.14, heading the national bowling averages?

3. Which bowler, who up until the beginning of the 1987 first-class season had taken 603 wickets (but scored only 310 runs) in a 226-match career for his county dating back to 1975, took the first hat-trick of his career in July 1987 against Middlesex at Lord's?

4. Which former England Test player, who took 703 wickets in a career for Middlesex lasting from 1949 to 1960, captaining them in the last three of those years, succeeded Colin Cowdrey as MCC President in 1987?

5. Which England opening bowler took 1,638 wickets between 1928 and 1947 but scored only 1,529 runs, his fifteen-match Test career yielding 68 wickets but just 28 runs?

6. Who, in a thirteen-year county career from 1948 to 1960, took 1,168 wickets at an average of 17.39, his best year being 1950 when he claimed 171 wickets in the County Championship and 193 overall, to head the national bowling averages and win the inaugural Young Cricketer of the Year Award?

7. Who took 100 wickets in a season in each of twenty consecutive years, failing to achieve this target only in his first and last season in County Championship cricket?

8. Who took 238 wickets at an average of 17.30 in 1947 when approaching his forty-seventh birthday, and in a career which began in 1922 and extended to 1952 claimed 2,979 victims, a record for a player still active in first-class cricket after the Second World War?

9. Who took 1,956 first-class wickets at an average of 14.90 in just ten seasons between 1930 and 1939?

10. Who was the Barbados-born medium-pace bowler who took 701 wickets for Glamorgan in 312 matches between 1963 and 1980?

44 *Test match bowling miscellany*

1. Who, at Melbourne in March 1979, took the last 7 Australian wickets in 33 balls, for the personal cost of one run, to finish with innings figures of 9–86, the first visiting bowler to take 9 wickets in a Test innings in Australia?

2. Who made his only Test appearance to date, for England against Australia at Trent Bridge in 1985, a split toe forcing him to retire from the match during his nineteenth over, his only victim having been night-watchman Bob Holland?

3. Who was the leading wicket-taker in the 1946–7 Ashes series, with 23 Australian wickets for 990 runs, the most runs conceded in a Test series by an English bowler?

4. Who was the left-arm bowler who conceded 298 runs in an innings when England compiled their mammoth 903–7 declared at The Oval in 1938?

5. Who made his début for Australia against England in 1920–21, at the age of thirty-four, taking 36 wickets for 946 runs in his first series, subsequently conceding 999 runs when capturing 24 England wickets in 1924–5, and ending his Test career at The Oval in 1926 with nine wickets in his last match, so taking his Test haul to 99 in twenty-one Tests?

6. Which Indian fast-medium bowler had a match analysis of 10–188 in the Third Test at Birmingham in 1986, the best figures by an Indian in a Test match in England?

7. Which Australian bowler took 5–103 and 5–146 in the Tied Test match in Madras in September 1986?

8. Who had innings figures of 6–16 when the West Indies were bowled out for 53, their lowest Test score, at Faisalabad in October 1986?

9. Which left-arm Indian spinner took 7–27 in Pakistan's first innings in the final Test, at Bangalore, in March 1987?

10. Who in 1987 became only the second England player to concede 200 runs in a Test innings, having an innings analysis of 3–217 as Pakistan scored their record 708 at The Oval?

45 *Leicestershire*

1. Who scored the only double century of his first-class career (to date) – 201* – for Leicestershire against Warwickshire at Edgbaston in August 1983?

2. Who was the Leicestershire bowler who took the first 9 Kent wickets at Grace Road in July 1985 and was on a hat-trick when the last Kent batsman came in, but bowled a no-ball and eventually had to settle for career-best figures of 9 for 70?

3. In which year did Leicestershire win the County Championship, their only success in the competition to date?

4. Which former Yorkshire player achieved the 'double' for Leicestershire in 1962, scoring 1,055 runs and taking exactly 100 wickets, the last time that this feat has been performed for the county?

5. Who played 493 matches for Leicestershire between 1950 and 1970, scored 23,662 runs (including a double century and a century in the same game on two occasions), held 427 catches and captained the county for four seasons in all?

6. Who was the forty-nine-year-old Leicestershire coach who in August 1986 took 5–22 in eleven overs against Yorkshire, this being his first county game for four seasons?

7. Who was the Leicestershire wicket-keeper who recorded 1,037 dismissals in first-class cricket stretching from 1965 to 1983, as well as playing in four Test matches in India in 1976–77, purely as a batsman, with Alan Knott keeping wicket?

8. Who made 423 appearances for Leicestershire between 1896 and 1923 and scored 21,872 runs, but is particularly remembered for 'carrying his bat' through a completed Leicestershire innings on seventeen occasions, including twice in the same match against Yorkshire in 1911?

9. Which Leicestershire bowler in 1929 achieved a then world record best innings analysis, when taking all 10 Glamorgan wickets for 18 runs?

10. Which Leicestershire pair, playing against Northamptonshire in August 1977, came together with the team's score at 45 for 9 and, scoring 119* and 98 respectively, added 228 for the last wicket, beating a county record set by Ewart Astill and William Marlow forty-four years previously?

46 *Benson and Hedges Cup*

1. Who, with 71 runs and three catches, won the Gold Award for Gloucestershire in their only Benson and Hedges Cup Final appearance, a 64-run victory over Kent in 1977?

2. Who in 1984 played for Warwickshire in their Benson and Hedges Cup Final defeat at the hands of Lancashire, having played in the inaugural final, between Leicestershire and Yorkshire, back in 1972?

3. Which overseas player, with more than 200 Test wickets to his credit, appeared in three out of the first four Benson and Hedges Cup finals?

4. Which Surrey bowler, playing against Nottinghamshire in the 1984 Benson and Hedges quarter-final, conceded 5 runs off his first six overs but 54 off his last four?

5. Who captained Yorkshire in the inaugural Benson and Hedges Cup Final at Lord's after Geoff Boycott had been sidelined by a finger injury sustained in a Gillette Cup match against Warwickshire?

6. Whose 107* for Kent against Middlesex at Lord's in April 1972 was the first century to be scored in the Benson and Hedges Cup?

7. What innovation was enacted in the Hampshire against Combined Universities Benson and Hedges Cup tie at Oxford in May 1987?

8. Which Somerset pair put on 269 together against Hampshire in May 1987, a new record partnership for the third wicket in any domestic one-day competition, a record held for five years by Essex's Graham Gooch and Keith Fletcher?

9. Who, playing for Leicestershire against Nottinghamshire in May 1987, took 4 wickets in six balls, including the hat-trick, the first hat-trick in the competition since Gladstone Small's, against Leicestershire, in 1984?

10. Who won the seventh Benson and Hedges Gold Award of his career when scoring 126* in a 1987 semi-final match at Canterbury?

47 *Test match miscellany*

1. Who became the first Sri Lankan batsman to record a Test century in Sri Lanka, when scoring 108 against New Zealand in Colombo in March 1984?

2. Who batted for 221 minutes over his 19* in the above match, enabling New Zealand to hold on for a draw?

3. Which England débutant retired hurt with a severe eye injury after being struck by Malcolm Marshall on the opening morning of the First Test at Edgbaston in June 1984, and has not subsequently regained his Test Match place?

4. Who in July 1984 returned to the England side for his eighteenth Test appearance, after an interval of eight years?

5. Who in fifty-eight Test matches for India achieved a world record by registering four 'pairs' in Test cricket?

6. Which England tail-ender, promoted to number three after the fall of an early wicket, scored 95 against Australia at Sydney in January 1983, an innings that saved his team from defeat?

7. Who played in fifty-eight Test matches for England over a record span of 30 years and 316 days?

8. Which brilliant Indian short-leg fielder held 53 catches in only twenty-seven Test matches between 1969 and 1977?

9. Who became the first player to score a double century and take 5 wickets in an innings of the same Test match, when scoring 219 and taking 5–56 for the West Indies against Australia in May 1955?

10. Which country in May 1985 suffered their first defeat against the West Indies in thirteen encounters dating back to March 1969?

48 *England v. Australia – Test miscellany*

1. Who made his only Test century, the highest innings of his first-class career, when scoring 185 against Australia at Sydney in January 1966, and sharing a 234-run opening partnership with Geoff Boycott, whose contribution was 84?

2. Who at Melbourne in February 1966 scored the only triple century in a Test match in Australia, his 307 against England lasting 727 minutes, the longest first-class innings in Australia?

3. Who began his controversial Test career at Trent Bridge in June 1964 against Australia, but had the misfortune to fracture a finger while fielding and was unable to bat in England's second innings?

4. Who scored his maiden Test century in his fifty-second innings, for Australia against England at Old Trafford in July 1964?

5. Which England batsman scored 256 in the above match, his tenth century in Test cricket but, remarkably, his first in a Test match in this country?

6. Who was the Australian off-break bowler who delivered 571 balls in England's innings in this same game, including one unbroken spell of 51 overs?

7. Who took 6–47 in England's first innings at The Oval in August 1964, but is chiefly remembered from this game because, when batting, he became Fred Trueman's 300th Test match 'victim'?

8. Who was the Australian fast bowler who made a highly successful Test match début at Lord's in 1961 when, two days before his twentieth birthday, he replaced injured tour captain, Richie Benaud; batting at number ten he scored 34 while the last two wickets were adding 102 runs, and in England's second innings he took 5–37 to set up a comfortable Australian victory?

9. Who helped to achieve an unlikely victory for Australia at Old Trafford in 1961 with a spell of 5–12 in twenty-five balls which was largely instrumental in reducing England from 150–1 to 201 all out?

10. Who took 104 Australian wickets in twenty-one Ashes Test matches between November 1946 and December 1954?

49 Middlesex

1. Which Middlesex batsman in August 1985 scored 201* at Lord's, the second man that season to score a double century for his county against the touring Australians, a feat that had previously only been accomplished once – in 1934?

2. Mike Gatting in 1984 became the first player to score 2,000 runs in a season for Middlesex since which player, twenty years previously?

3. Who in 1978 was the last Middlesex bowler to take 100 first-class wickets in a season prior to John Emburey in 1983?

4. Which son of a former Test cricketer played just one season for Middlesex in 1980, his 85 Championship wickets at an average of 14.72 being instrumental in the county winning the Championship?

5. Who made 642 appearances for Middlesex between 1949 and 1982, becoming the only post-war cricketer to play in the County Championship in five different decades?

6. Who scored 331* in a day, for Middlesex against Worcestershire at Worcester in 1949, the highest innings in a post-war County Championship match, prior to 1988?

7. Who has scored a record 40,302 runs for Middlesex, his 119 centuries also remaining a county record?

8. Which Norfolk-born batsman scored 21,302 runs and held 452 catches in 387 appearances for Middlesex between 1956 and 1972, captaining the county immediately prior to Mike Brearley?

9. Which wicket-keeper between 1938 and 1956 recorded 595 dismissals for Middlesex, 464 catches and 131 stumpings?

10. Who was the Australian-born Oxford Blue who became captain of Middlesex in 1963 at just twenty-four years of age, but retired at the end of the 1964 season, having made just ninety-two appearances for the county over a span of seven years?

50 *Test match batting miscellany*

1. Who was stuck on 98 not out when England recorded a nine-wicket victory over South Africa at Old Trafford in June 1951, just missing the opportunity of becoming the first player to score his 100th first-class century in a Test match?

2. Who in December 1975 was the first Australian to score a century on his Test début against opposition other than England?

3. Who became the first player to score at least 150 in both innings of the same Test match, hitting 150* and 153 against Pakistan at Lahore in 1980?

4. Which recently retired player scored twelve Test match hundreds, exceeding 150 on eight occasions, and progressing to four double centuries?

5. Who scored 20* and 74 for India against Australia at Calcutta in January 1960, becoming in the process the first player to bat on all five days of a Test match?

6. Who are the only father and son to have carried their bats through completed Test innings?

7. Which England batsman, having already been dismissed for scores of 98 and 96 in Tests, was out for 99, caught at the wicket, against South Africa at Lord's in June 1960 and, in his fourth Test after this mishap, was run out for 99 against Pakistan at Lahore in October 1961?

8. Who holds the record for the most boundaries scored in a Test innings, 5 sixes and 52 fours?

9. Who, between 3 January and 2 May 1983, scored 1,065 runs in nine Test matches against Pakistan and the West Indies, setting a new record for the earliest date by which 1,000 Test runs have been made in a calendar year?

10. Which current South Australian batsman, with twenty-seven Test appearances to his credit, made his highest Test score of 159 in his début innings, for Australia against Pakistan at Perth in November 1983?

51 *Former players with more than one county*

1. Who was the opening batsman who played 135 games for Lancashire between 1959 and 1967, before moving to Gloucestershire, where he made eighty-one appearances between 1968 and 1971?

2. Which county did former Northamptonshire and England captain Freddie Brown represent from 1931 to 1948?

3. Which opening batsman, who made seven Test appearances, played 107 games for Yorkshire between 1956 and 1962, 269 games for Nottinghamshire between 1963 and 1972, and 64 games for Derbyshire between 1973 and 1975, being capped by all three counties, also captaining Nottinghamshire in 1972 before assuming the same role at Derbyshire?

4. Which slow left-arm bowler, who played in two Tests against the West Indies in 1950, became the first cricketer to be capped by three different counties, playing 93 games for Lancashire between 1948 and 1954, 94 for Worcestershire between 1955 and 1958 and 54 for Derbyshire between 1959 and 1962?

5. Which county did C. B. Fry occasionally represent between 1909 and 1921, having previously made 236 appearances for Sussex?

6. Which county did former England off-break bowler, Jim Laker, represent as an amateur from 1962 to 1964?

7. Who was the England all-rounder who made 404 appearances for Warwickshire between 1923 and 1939 before transferring to Worcestershire in 1946, when almost forty-five years old, and playing eighty-six matches up to 1951?

8. Which county did former England and Lancashire fast bowler Ken Shuttleworth represent between 1977 and 1980?

9. Which future England batsman surprisingly moved to Northamptonshire in 1955 after winning Championship medals with Surrey in the previous two seasons?

10. Which England opening batsman made 161 appearances for Worcestershire and 162 appearances for Kent in a first-class career which began in 1949 and ended in 1965?

52 *England all-rounders*

1. Who made his Test début in November 1984 in the country of his father's birth, bowled Kapil Dev in his first over, but was rather less successful as the series wore on, scoring 96 runs at 19.20 and taking 4 wickets at 72.00 in what are still his only Test appearances?

2. Which Old Harrovian won four Blues at Cambridge between 1890 and 1893, twenty England caps between 1893 and 1905, five as captain, scoring 1,415 runs and taking 24 wickets, and in later years was to survive an assassination attempt when Governor of Bengal?

3. Which player, in thirty-nine Test appearances, is the only man to have a highest score for England of exactly 100 not out, scored in less than two hours against South Africa at Lord's in 1929, though he is better known as a bowler, having taken 155 wickets in Test cricket?

4. Which all-rounder, on his England début against Pakistan at Lord's in June 1971, opened England's second innings with Brian Luckhurst, not having batted in the first, and scored 58* in an unbroken partnership of 117?

5. Which all-rounder opened the England innings with Geoff Boycott at Trent Bridge in June 1964, after John Edrich had withdrawn from the match through injury?

6. Which great English batsman achieved his best Test match bowling figures of 5–36 against South Africa at Johannesburg in December 1926, in the very first of his eighty-five international appearances?

7. Who, in twenty-nine Test matches between December 1961 and August 1969, had a best score of 127 and a best innings bowling analysis of 4–38?

8. Which man, playing against Australia at Brisbane in December 1936, aggregated 102 runs in addition to taking 8 wickets for the second successive Test, his previous Test, against India, having yielded his best Test innings figures of 7–80?

9. Who took Australia's first 4 wickets at Sydney in February 1902, with just 48 runs on the board, and six months later at The Oval played one of the most remarkable of all Test innings when hitting 104 in eighty-five minutes, having come in at 48–5 with a further 215 needed for victory, the target being finally reached with just one wicket in hand?

10. Who made his England Test début at the age of thirty-four and, in a forty-four-match Test career, finished with 2,484 runs at an average of 40.06, including five centuries, and 47 wickets from his often under-used medium-pace bowling?

53 *Northamptonshire*

1. Who hit his only three-figure score of the season, a career-best 234 which included 12 sixes and 25 fours, for Northamptonshire against Gloucestershire in May 1986, his first innings of the season for the county?

2. Who was the twenty-two-year-old Northamptonshire batsman who in 1986 scored 224* against Glamorgan and 200* against Yorkshire?

3. Who scored 106 for Northamptonshire against Hampshire in May 1985 on his Championship début, having replaced injured captain Geoff Cook in the team only twenty-five minutes before the start of play?

4. Who in 1984 followed John Timms, Dennis Brookes and Brian Reynolds as the fourth man to make 400 appearances for Northamptonshire?

5. Which three players were all official captains of Northamptonshire during the 1975 first-class season?

6. Who was the Australian all-rounder who, between 1952 and 1959, achieved the 'double' for Northamptonshire on a record seven occasions?

7. Which overseas player, in 262 appearances for Northamptonshire between 1964 and 1977, scored 15,961 runs, took 551 wickets and held 175 catches?

8. Who would have taken particular delight from scoring 300 for Northamptonshire against Surrey at The Oval in 1958, the highest individual Championship innings for the county?

9. Which Northamptonshire batsman, playing against Hampshire at Southampton in April 1987, reached 20,000 first-class runs in his career, sixteen years after his début?

10. Against which county, in 1907, were Northamptonshire dismissed for 12, the record lowest innings score in the history of the County Championship?

54 *Test match miscellany*

1. Who, in only his third Test match, scored 210* for Pakistan against Australia at Faisalabad in March 1980, the highest score in Test cricket by a wicket-keeper?

2. Who bowled twelve overs for Australia in the course of ninety-six Test matches, ten of them in this Faisalabad game, and the other two also against Pakistan, at Melbourne in December 1983, his penultimate Test appearance?

3. Who is the only England captain to gain five victories in a single Test series in Australia?

4. Who was the Australian captain who scored 121 of his team's total of 198 in the first innings of the Sixth Test against England at Sydney in February 1979?

5. Who scored 250 for the West Indies against India at Kanpur in February 1979, his only century in nineteen Test matches?

6. Who carried his bat for 99* when England were dismissed for 215 in the Perth Test Match in December 1979, a game they lost by 138 runs?

7. Who became the first player to bat throughout both completed innings of a Test match when scoring 55 and 105 in the match between New Zealand and the West Indies at Dunedin in February 1980, being the last man out in each innings?

8. Who in March 1981 became the first black West Indian to play in a Test match for England, ironically against the West Indies in Barbados?

9. Who in 1981 took a record 42 wickets in an Ashes series for Australia in the six-Test series in England?

10. Who, in February 1982 in his fifty-ninth and final Test match, captained England in Colombo, in the first official Test match played by Sri Lanka?

55 One-day cricket – The Sunday League

1. Which two players in 1984 reached 300 wickets in the Sunday league on the same day, and when the John Player League ended in 1986 they were still level with a record 344 victims each?

2. Which bowler made a record 261 appearances in the John Player League and ironically took 261 wickets?

3. Which county lost their first 4 wickets for no runs, and 6 wickets for four runs, against Surrey at The Oval in 1978, before the tail batted through the forty overs to reach 99?

4. Which eighteen-year-old Surrey bowler, in his first game of the season, and only his fifth first team appearance, took the first 4 wickets in the above match?

5. Only two players have been dismissed 'obstructing the field' in John Player League matches, both wicket-keepers: Derek Taylor became the second in 1980, but which England Test player had been the first, when playing against Middlesex eight years earlier?

6. Which player, in a career with two counties, was the only non-wicket-keeper to take 100 catches in the John Player League?

7. Who scored nine centuries in the John Player League up to 1977, a total that was not overtaken until 1986?

8. Which two counties achieved the highest match aggregate in the John Player League when both reached 300 runs in their 1985 encounter?

9. Which two players shared the record partnership in the John Player League, adding 273 runs for the second wicket against Nottinghamshire in 1983, advancing their team to a final total of 306–2?

10. Which wicket-keeper made a record 236 dismissals in the John Player League, including 49 stumpings?

56 *Australian tours to England*

1. Which member of the 1977 Australian tour party had played in 46 matches for Somerset in 1971 and 1972?

2. Which Australian Test player, on his only tour of England, was vice-captain to Ian Chappel in 1972?

3. Who scored 345 in 205 minutes before tea for the Australians against Nottinghamshire at Trent Bridge in 1921, the most runs ever scored by an individual in a day and the highest score by a tourist to England?

4. Which Australian tourist headed the national batting averages in 1953, scoring an aggregate of 102 runs and losing his wicket just once in seventeen innings for an average of 102.00?

5. Which English county has beaten the touring Australians on a record nine occasions?

6. Who played in fourteen Tests for Australia between 1946 and 1950 before signing for Somerset, for whom he was to score 116 against the 1956 Australian tourists?

7. Which Australian bowler, with 10–37 at Sheffield in 1930, was the last player to take 10 wickets in an innings in a match against Yorkshire?

8. Which legendary star of the 'Golden Age' made his highest score, 300*, for the Australians against Sussex at Hove on their 1899 tour?

9. Frederick Spofforth in 1884 became the first Australian tourist to exceed 200 wickets in an English season, 207 at 12.82; but who, four years later, became the only other to achieve the feat, his haul of 283 being only ever bettered by two players?

10. Which seven Australian players all averaged over 50 on the 1948 tour of England, aggregating over 10,800 runs between them?

57 Nottinghamshire

1. Which twenty-two-year-old opening bat, standing in because Chris Broad and Tim Robinson were on Test duty, became the second youngest player to score a double century for the county when scoring 203* against Derbyshire in July 1987?

2. Who scored a career-best 210* for Nottinghamshire against Middlesex at Lord's in August 1984, his first century being completed in just ninety-four balls, though he slowed down considerably thereafter?

3. At which venue, outside the county boundary, did Nottinghamshire play their John Player League game against Middlesex in September 1983?

4. Whom did Clive Rice replace as Nottinghamshire captain in July 1979, fifteen months later than anticipated, following the cancellation of his original appointment in April 1978 because of his contract with Kerry Packer's World Series Cricket?

5. In 1984 Richard Hadlee became the first player to take 100 wickets in a season for Nottinghamshire since which bowler, seventeen years previously, in 1967?

6. In this same season, 1984, Hadlee also became only the second post-war Nottinghamshire cricketer to perform the 'double' of 1,000 runs and 100 wickets, emulating which fellow Australasian who scored 1,517 runs and took 136 wickets in 1957?

7. Who made 257 appearances as Nottinghamshire's wicket-keeper between 1957 and 1965, scoring 7,410 runs and claiming 598 dismissals in a career that also saw him playing in six Test matches for England?

8. Who were the two brothers who played a combined total of 1,072 matches for Nottinghamshire and, between them, scored nearly 55,000 runs?

9. Who, between 1924 and 1938, took 1,247 wickets for Nottinghamshire at an average of only 16.24, heading the national first-class bowling averages on five occasions?

10. Who was the Nottinghamshire captain between 1919 and 1934, leading the side to the County Championship in 1929, their last title prior to the Clive Rice and Richard Hadlee inspired successes of the 1980s?

58 *England v. Australia – Test miscellany*

1. Who shared a record fifth-wicket partnership of 405 with Don Bradman for Australia against England at Sydney in December 1946, both batsmen coincidentally finishing up with the same score?

2. Who bowled Don Bradman first ball at the Melbourne Cricket Ground in December 1932, in the great batsman's first innings in the infamous 'Bodyline' series?

3. Which England spin bowler demonstrated his ability as a batsman when making 63, his highest Test score, in an 89–run ninth-wicket partnership with Alec Bedser at Trent Bridge in June 1948, more than doubling England's first innings total in the process?

4. Who scored 30 out of England's total of 52 in the first innings of the final Test at The Oval in 1948, being last man out after opening the batting?

5. Who bowled Don Bradman for 0 with the second ball he received in his final Test Match innings at The Oval in 1948, thereby restricting him to four short of the aggregate 7,000 runs he required to establish a career Test match average of 100?

6. Len Hutton carried his bat for 156* in the Fourth Test of the 1950–51 Ashes series, but which Englishman finished up with an identical score, also not out, in the Fifth and final Test, his only century against Australia and accomplished on his thirty-first birthday?

7. When Len Hutton carried his bat for 156* in this February 1951 Adelaide Test, which Australian opener almost achieved the same feat but was dismissed for 206 runs, scored out of a total of 371?

8. Which Australian made his Test début in the same match as Geoff Boycott and was to dismiss the Yorkshireman in his first three Test innings, each time caught at slip by Bobby Simpson?

9. Who, after scoring 72 in the final match of the 1954–55 Ashes series at Sydney, allowed himself to be bowled in order to present Ray Lindwall with his 100th wicket in Australia v. England Tests, but four years later, opening the England innings at Melbourne in his last Test match, was dismissed twice without scoring by a less sympathetic Lindwall?

10. Which Australian bowler achieved his best innings analysis in Tests, 6–38, when England were dismissed for 87 at Melbourne in January 1959?

59 *University cricket*

1. Who played his only match for Middlesex in 1977 against Cambridge University at Fenners, a year before going on to Oxford University, where between 1978 and 1983 he was to play against Cambridge on six more occasions and become the first man to appear in six Varsity matches?

2. Who achieved the unusual distinction of playing for Cambridge University against Oxford in the 1975 and 1976 Varsity matches and for Oxford against Cambridge in 1978?

3. Who were the two players, one from Derbyshire and the other from Warwickshire, who scored centuries on their first-class débuts, both in 1971 and both against Oxford University?

4. Which player, capped twice by the West Indies, once each on successive MCC tours in 1947–48 and 1953–54, became in 1956 the oldest player to have appeared in the Varsity match, when opening the bowling for Oxford at the age of thirty-nine?

5. In rather more successful days for the universities, against which county did Cambridge University score 703–9 declared in 1890, the record score in the second innings of an English domestic match?

6. Which batsman scored an all-time record of 3,319 runs for Oxford University when winning four Blues between 1934 and 1937, during which time he made his one and only England appearance, against South Africa at Trent Bridge in 1935, scoring 5 in his only innings?

7. Which Cambridge University freshman, who was to play six games for Somerset during vacations, became in 1961 the only university bowler to take all ten wickets in an innings against a county side when taking 10–78 against Leicestershire at Loughborough?

8. Which Cambridge University undergraduate, now a leading journalist, performed the hat-trick against Essex in May 1952?

9. Which Cambridge University undergraduate carried his bat for 80* out of 163 against the 1938 Australians, helping to earn himself selection for the winter tour of South Africa, where he was to score 93 and 106 on his Test début?

10. Which Cambridge University bowler played just twice for Kent in 1926, the same year in which he finished off Oxford's first innings in the Varsity match with a hat-trick?

60 *Test cricket firsts – Batting*

1. Who was the Oxford University freshman who in 1959 became the first post-war player to score a century against England, in England, on his Test match début, when scoring 112 in his country's second innings at Old Trafford?

2. Which England player, at Port-of-Spain in April 1974, became the first person in Test history to score 99 and a century in the same Test match?

3. Who is the only Englishman to have a top score of 99 in Test cricket, scored against South Africa at Trent Bridge in 1947?

4. Who made his Test début in November 1969 against Australia at Kanpur, scoring a duck in the first innings, but in the second innings becoming only the sixth Indian to score a century on his Test début and the first of any nationality to combine the feat with a duck?

5. Which English player, with scores of 176 and 127 against Australia at Melbourne in 1924–25, became the first man to score over 300 runs in a Test match without the aid of a double century?

6. Which Australian batsman became, in 1926, the first player to score three Test centuries in a series in England, when in successive innings he accumulated 133* at Lord's, 151 at Headingley and 109 at Old Trafford?

7. Which player scored 558 runs in the 1968–69 New Zealand against West Indies series, the first man to score 500 or more runs in a post-war three-Test series?

8. Which man in January 1957 became the first to be given out 'handled the ball' in a Test match, having in 1951 been the obstructed fielder when Len Hutton became the first player to be out 'obstructing the field' in a Test?

9. Which player, coming in with England's score at 138–5, scored 102* out of 133 as the total was advanced to 271, to record the first Test century at St John's, Antigua, in March 1981?

10. Who, playing against Pakistan at Eden Gardens, Calcutta, in December 1952 and batting at number eight, scored 110, the second Indian after Lala Amarnath to score a century on his Test début and the first to do so in his first innings, yet he was only to appear in two more Tests?

61 *Somerset*

1. At which venue in June 1987 did Somerset become the fifth different first-class county to lose to Minor County opposition in the Gillette Cup/NatWest Trophy?

2. Which Somerset batsman, when scoring 206* against Warwickshire at Edgbaston on 1 July, became the first player to reach 1,000 first-class runs in the 1987 season?

3. Who carried his bat for 165* out of 300 against Hampshire in August 1987, the first Somerset player to achieve the feat in a County Championship match since Philip Slocombe did so twice during the 1978 season?

4. Who on 1 June 1985 made the highest score in county cricket for thirty-six years, when scoring 322 for Somerset against Warwickshire, facing 258 balls in 294 minutes and hitting 8 sixes and 42 fours?

5. Which Somerset bowler took 100 wickets in first-class cricket in 1978 at an average of 16.40?

6. When Bill Alley became, in 1961, the last man to score over 3,000 runs in a first-class season, 2,761 being scored in the County Championship alone, which other Somerset player scored over 2,000 Championship runs in the season?

7. Who in 1935 was the twenty-year-old, making his Championship début for Somerset against Essex at Frome, who scored a century in sixty-three minutes, the fastest of the season, and in 329 matches up to 1954 became the county's leading scorer with 21,142 runs?

8. Who was the slow left-arm bowler who, between 1909 and 1937, took a record 2,166 wickets for Somerset, also scoring 11,385 runs and holding a record 381 catches for the county?

9. Who was the Durham-born wicket-keeper who recorded 1,007 dismissals for Somerset between 1948 and 1964, scored over 12,000 runs and captained the county for the five seasons immediately prior to retiring?

10. Who made 287 appearances for Somerset between 1898 and 1927, being captain for two periods totalling a record thirteen seasons, and also captained England six times at Rugby Union football?

62 *England v. Pakistan*

1. Who was the Pakistan opening bowler who broke captain Mike Brearley's left arm in a one-day match immediately prior to the Third Test Match at Karachi in January 1978, Brearley having to return home and miss the subsequent tour to New Zealand?

2. Which Glamorgan off-spinner made two appearances for England against Pakistan in 1954 and toured Australia and New Zealand the following winter, but played in only five games and never appeared in another Test?

3. Which Pakistani made his Test début at Trent Bridge in July 1954, at the age of 16 years and 352 days, bowled both England's century-makers, Reg Simpson (101) and Denis Compton (278), but never played in another Test?

4. Who claimed the first six Pakistan wickets to fall at Headingley in July 1987 and, although ending with a personal Test match best of 8–107, could not prevent an innings defeat for England?

5. Who, batting at either number seven or number eight and selected principally as a bowler, scored 218 runs for England in three Tests against Pakistan in March 1984 at an average of 43.60, but took only four wickets in the series at an average of 65.00?

6. Who came to the wicket at The Oval in 1967 with Pakistan's second innings score at 53–7 and proceeded to score 146 in 200 minutes, sharing in a ninth-wicket stand of 190 with Intikhab Alam which remains a world record?

7. Who in only his second Test match scored 274 for Pakistan at Edgbaston in June 1971, the first double century for his country in Tests against England?

8. Who had match figures of 13–71 against Pakistan at Lord's in 1974, his eight-wicket haul in the second innings including a spell of 6 for 2 in fifty-one balls, after water had seeped through the covers during a storm?

9. Which England batsman scored 111 in the Third and final Test at Karachi in February 1962, and four months later in his own and England's next innings scored 101* at Edgbaston against the same opposition, sharing in an unbroken sixth-wicket partnership of 153 with David Allen, a record for England v. Pakistan Tests which still stands?

10. What unusual feat was achieved by Pakistan's Mohammad Ghazali in the course of his second and final Test, against England at Old Trafford in July 1954?

63 *Gillette Cup/NatWest Trophy*

1. Against which county were Worcestershire playing when they amassed an English limited-overs record 404–3, Graeme Hick scoring 172*, in their NatWest Trophy first round match in June 1987?

2. Which former county colleague's record in the sixty-over competition did Derek Underwood surpass when taking 8–31 in Kent's first round NatWest Trophy match against Scotland in June 1987?

3. Which Minor County bowler, who made his Test début for Australia at Wellington in February 1986, was the first to complete two five-wicket hauls in the NatWest Trophy: 5–51 against Surrey in 1982 and 7–32 against Lancashire in 1983, his side losing both matches?

4. Who scored 67 in the 1984 NatWest Trophy Final and was voted Man of the Match, becoming the first player to be so assessed in Gillette, Benson and Hedges and NatWest Trophy finals?

5. Who scored 141* in Sussex's Gillette Cup quarter-final victory over Warwickshire in 1980, the last century to be scored in the Gillette Cup and the fifth highest score in the competition's eighteen-year history?

6. Off which seasoned Test bowler did David Hughes score 26 in the last over of Lancashire's innings in the 1976 Gillette Cup Final, a match they were to lose by 4 wickets?

7. Which player in 1974 became the first to win the Man of the Match award in the same year's Gillette Cup semi-final and final, respectively scoring 20 against Somerset and 18* against Lancashire, and not bowling in either game?

8. Which Minor County in 1974 became the second to dismiss first-class opposition from the Gillette Cup when overcoming Glamorgan at Swansea by 6 wickets, before losing to Surrey in the second round?

9. Which bowler, playing for Northamptonshire against Sussex in 1963, became the first player to perform the hat-trick in the Gillette Cup?

10. Whose 132 for Lincolnshire against Northumberland in 1971 remains as the highest score by a Minor County batsman in the Gillette Cup or NatWest Trophy?

64 *Gentlemen v. Players*

1. In which year was the last ever Gentlemen v. Players match contested?

2. Who were the two captains in this final Gentlemen v. Players match, both now associated with the BBC's Test match coverage?

3. Twenty of the twenty-two players on the final Gentleman v. Players fixture played Test cricket during their careers. Which two members of the Gentlemen's side, both Cambridge Blues, never attained that status?

4. Of the twenty internationals to appear in the last Gentlemen v. Players match, who was the only non-Englishman, a South African then at Oxford University, who was to play eight times for his country between 1963 and 1967, his début coinciding with that of Graeme Pollock and his last match being Mike Proctor's first?

5. Which England captain, representing the Gentlemen in the 1950 match, scored 122 out of 131 during his 110-minute stay at the crease?

6. Who was the long-serving Hampshire opening bowler and middle order batsman who took all 10 wickets for 37 runs for the Players against the Gentlemen at The Oval in 1927?

7. Who was the nineteen-year-old, Scottish-born leg-spinner, a future international, who made his first-class début in this same match and took the first wicket to fall when bowling Andy Sandham, the Players' opening batsman?

8. Who captained the Players to victory over the Gentlemen at Lord's in 1937, and the Gentlemen to victory over the Players at the same venue in 1938?

9. Which member of the Players side, at Scarborough in 1925, scored 266*, the highest score in a Gentlemen v. Players match?

10. Which man scored 232* in the 1903 Gentlemen v. Players match, the highest score by an amateur and the highest score in Gentlemen v. Players matches at Lord's?

65 *Surrey*

1. Who in August 1985 was rushed to Derby to replace the indisposed Trevor Jesty and, having arrived at lunchtime on the first day, batted at number seven and scored 143, his maiden century in his sixth first-class innings?

2. Who in 1980 took 121 wickets for Surrey at an average of 15.40, putting him in third place in the national bowling averages?

3. Which Surrey player, batting at number nine against Glamorgan in June 1981, scored his maiden first-class century in sixty-two minutes, winning the Lawrence Trophy for the fastest century of the season?

4. Which Surrey bowler, playing against Sussex at Eastbourne in August 1972, took 4 wickets in four balls, the first man to perform the feat in England since 1956, going on to make it 5 in six, and when Udaykumar Joshi was run out off the next ball 6 wickets had fallen from his last seven balls?

5. Who captained Surrey from 1952 to 1956, leading the county to the Championship in all five seasons?

6. Which inspirational and inventive captain of the interwar years led Surrey between 1921 and 1931, a period during which perfect Oval batting tracks conspired to prevent the county from actually winning the Championship, though they were never to finish outside the top ten?

7. Who was the famous Surrey and England wicket-keeper whose 1,223 career dismissals between 1902 and 1927, constituted a world record that was to stand for nearly fifty years?

8. Who scored 36,175 runs for Surrey, including 88 centuries, and in 1897 became the first player to achieve the 'double' of 1,000 runs and 100 wickets in a season for the county?

9. Who was the Surrey and England fast bowler who, between 1894 and 1897, took 888 wickets for the county over the first four seasons, half of his record career haul of 1,775 dismissals?

10. Who scored 357* against Somerset at The Oval in 1899, still the highest individual innings for Surrey and setting world records which also still remain – the highest score by a player 'carrying his bat' through a completed innings, and the highest total of runs added (811) within the duration of one individual innings?

66 *England v. Australia – Test miscellany*

1. Denis Compton and Bill Edrich are remembered as the pair who scored the winning runs at The Oval in 1953, regaining the Ashes for England after nineteen years, but which combination set up the victory by sharing all Australia's second innings wickets?

2. Which twenty-one-year-old, playing in his first Test match for Australia, scored 71 out of an unbeaten third-wicket stand of 89 which clinched an eight-wicket victory over England at Brisbane in December 1958?

3. In 'Jim Laker's Test Match' at Old Trafford in 1956 which Australian batsman scored 89, his country's second highest individual innings in the five-match series?

4. Who, at Headingley in 1956, returned to the England side at the age of forty-one, after a five-and-a-half-year absence, and scored 98, sharing in a partnership of 187 with Peter May to rescue England from the perilous position of 17–3?

5. Who was selected for England against Australia at Old Trafford in 1956, his first Test match for two years, having played only four previous first-class innings in the season, though his 113 was to prove him an inspired selection?

6. Who, playing only as a replacement for the injured Tom Graveney, held five catches off Jim Laker's bowling in the Old Trafford Test of 1956?

7. Who was 98 not out at lunch on the first day of the 1938 Trent Bridge Test Match, completing his century off the first ball after the interval, and finally contributing 126 runs to England's total of 658?

8. Who scored 102 in the above innings and, at 20 years and 19 days, remains the youngest player to score a century for England?

9. Who, again in this same match, replied for Australia by unfolding one of the great innings in Test match history, 232 scored out of 300 in under four hours, his final 72 coming in 28 minutes, in a last-wicket partnership of 77 with Leslie Fleetwood-Smith?

10. Whose score stood at 169* when England's innings was declared at 903–7 at The Oval in 1938, this being the only one of his four Test centuries to be scored in an Ashes Test?

67 Career statistics – All-rounders

1. Which post-war England captain, a left-hand batsman and right-arm bowler, scored 34,994 first-class runs at 33.26, the most by a player who never scored a double century, and took 1,168 wickets at 26.40 in a twenty-nine-year career that covered two counties?

2. Which famous all-rounder boasts the following impressive career statistics: 58,969 first-class runs, second only to Jack Hobbs, at 40.75, with a top score of 305* for MCC against Tasmania at Hobart; 2,068 first-class wickets at 19.85, though he hardly bowled during the last ten years of his career; and a world record 1,018 catches by an outfielder, all in a career that spanned the years 1906 to 1938?

3. Who, between 1904 and 1906, was the first man to achieve the 'double' of 2,000 runs and 100 wickets in three successive seasons?

4. Who scored 17,039 runs at 27.30 and took 462 wickets at 30.87 between 1954 and 1972, in a first-class career in England (with Warwickshire), New Zealand (with Otago) and Australia (with Tasmania), but won four Test caps for another country altogether, scoring 166 against Australia on his Test début?

5. Which Peruvian-born cricketer scored 13,325 runs, took 1,221 wickets and held 212 catches in a career which extended from 1930 to 1961, during which period he performed the 'double' on two occasions, in 1932 and 1949, for different counties?

6. Which overseas player scored 21,748 runs and took 1,395 wickets between 1965 and 1981, recording 100 wickets in a season twice and 1,000 runs on nine occasions, though he failed to harness the two and was never to achieve the 'double'?

7. Which three post-war England all-rounders have scored over 20,000 runs and taken over 2,000 wickets in their first-class careers?

8. Who took 496 wickets and scored 10,776 runs in a career of 332 first-class matches for two counties between 1960 and 1978, a rather erratic career which only really burst into life in 1966, when he performed the 'double'?

9. Which two great all-rounders, born in the same village just six years apart, batted right-handed and bowled left, and cumulatively scored 76,325 runs and took 6,920 wickets, performing 'the double' on thirty occasions between them?

10. Which Hampshire pair jointly recorded nearly 32,000 runs and 4,900 wickets, performing 'the double' five times each between 1921 and 1930, both together in 1921, 1923 and 1928?

68 *England Captains*

1. Which captain led England in nineteen home Tests without defeat, these including two series against Australia?

2. Which current player captained England in twelve Test matches, nine against the West Indies, and three against Australia, failing to win any of them?

3. Who in 1966 took over the England captaincy for the final Test against the West Indies, when England gained some consolation for the loss of the series with an innings victory? Continuing in charge the following year, he won five matches out of six against India and Pakistan, so achieving six wins and one draw in his seven Test matches as captain.

4. Who during 1972 and 1973 captained England in the first eight of his nine Test appearances?

5. Who captained England in twenty-seven Test matches but was never asked to lead a tour of Australia, where, remarkably, he was vice-captain on four separate visits?

6. Who in sixty-six Test match appearances captained England a record forty-one times?

7. Who played in just two Tests for England, these coming on the 1951–52 tour of India, captaining the side in the second of these, at Madras, when India recorded their first victory in Test cricket?

8. Who captained England against the West Indies in 1939, the last Test series before the outbreak of war, and was also in charge against India in 1946, the first series after the resumption of peace?

9. Who captained England in twenty-two Test matches between 1897 and 1909, all of them against Australia, this being a record number for either country in the long-running series of Ashes Tests?

10. Which player was vice-captain to Douglas Jardine on the infamous 'Bodyline' tour of Australia in 1932–33, having captained England himself the last time that the two countries had met, at The Oval in 1930?

69 *Sussex*

1. Who are the two brothers who shared an unbeaten partnership of 303 for Sussex against Kent in July 1987, breaking the county's record 'brotherly' partnership of 297, previously held by Harry and Jim Parks from 1937?

2. Who are the two brothers who, together, aggregated 1,189 appearances for Sussex and scored over 63,000 runs?

3. Who were the two brothers who were to captain both Sussex and England in the years between 1922 and 1930?

4. Who took 464 wickets for Sussex in a career that stretched from 1969 to 1980, and was the only player to appear in all three Gillette Cup finals which the county reached in the 1970s?

5. Which three players represented Sussex in a Gillette Cup final, having all played in the final for another county thirteen years earlier?

6. Which medium-pace seamer was the last bowler to take all 10 wickets in an innings in an English first-class match, taking 10–49 against Warwickshire at Worthing in 1964, though Sussex lost the match by 182 runs when bowled out for 23 in their second innings?

7. Who was the future captain of South Africa who led Sussex in 1934 and 1935 and, in five seasons with the county, scored nearly 5,000 runs and took 38 wickets?

8. Who was the legendary Sussex seam bowler who took 2,211 wickets for the county, scored over 17,000 runs and achieved the 'double' on seven occasions?

9. Who was the fifty-two-year-old who took 17 Warwickshire wickets for 106 runs at Horsham in 1926, the only Sussex bowler to obtain so many wickets in a Championship match?

10. Who, in 294 innings for Sussex between 1895 and 1920, scored 18,594 runs including 58 centuries, at an average of 63.24, and once achieved the unparalleled feat of scoring two separate first-class centuries on the same day, 22 August 1896, against Yorkshire?

70 *Gillette Cup/NatWest Trophy*

1. Which county captain carried his bat for 16* out of 83 in his county's second round NatWest Trophy match against Yorkshire at Headingley in July 1987, the lowest score by a batsman carrying his bat since Kent's Peter Hearn scored 12* out of 32 against Hampshire in 1952?

2. Who in July 1987 partially rescued a previously rather grim bowling analysis by taking a hat-trick in his twelfth and final over, finishing with 3–73 in Derbyshire's losing NatWest quarter-final at the hands of Nottinghamshire, Bruce French becoming the third victim in a hat-trick for the second time in seven weeks?

3. Who dismissed Clive Lloyd for no score in the 1986 NatWest Trophy Final, the great West Indian's last appearance for Lancashire?

4. Who, with an innings of 206 against Oxfordshire in a NatWest Trophy match in 1984, became the first player to score a double century in limited-overs cricket?

5. Who scored 24* and took 6 wickets for 29 runs in the 1979 Gillette Cup Final, but failed to win the Man of the Match award, which went to Viv Richards?

6. Who achieved an average of 112.66 in Gillette Cup matches, without the aid of a century, totalling 676 runs in twelve innings, in six of which he was not dismissed?

7. Which former England seam bowler took a record 81 wickets in the Gillette Cup between 1963 and 1980?

8. Who in the 1971 final took a memorable catch to dismiss Asif Iqbal for 89, a decisive factor in ensuring that Lancashire retained the Gillette Cup?

9. Who scored 146 in the 1965 Gillette Cup Final, the highest individual score in a final of the competition?

10. Who scored the first century in the Gillette Cup, scoring 121 runs for Lancashire against his future county, Leicestershire, in May 1963?

71 High scores – Individual

1. Which batsman twice scored over 3,000 runs in a first-class season before anyone else achieved the feat, scoring 3,159 at 63.18 in 1899, and 3,065 at 87.57 in 1900?

2. Which England batsman and part-time bowler scored a career-best 240* against Gloucestershire in 1974, nine years after taking the only hat-trick of his career against the same county?

3. Which player in June 1981 became the first to score 1,000 first-class runs in a month since former England captain Mike Smith hit 1,209 in July 1959?

4. Who scored a record 1,294 first-class runs in a month in June 1949, following this up with 1,050 runs in August of that year, to finish the season with 3,429 runs, at an average of 68.58?

5. Who scored 307 for the MCC against South Australia in December 1962, the highest innings ever played by a touring player in Australia, and also the personal best by this formidable batsman in his long and distinguished career?

6. Which twenty-three-year-old, playing on his home ground, scored 214 and 100* on his Test Match début in February 1972?

7. Who exceeded 200 on six occasions in the course of ten centuries in England in the summer of 1930?

8. Who at Hove in May 1930, scored a county record 333 for Sussex against Northamptonshire, eclipsing the county's previous best, 285*, set by his uncle in 1901?

9. Who in December 1903 became the first player to score over 300 runs in a Test match, when on his début for England he recorded 287 and 19 against Australia at Sydney?

10. Who, between June 1986 and March 1987, scored 1,326 runs in thirteen completed innings against England, Australia, Sri Lanka and Pakistan, for a batting average of 102.00?

72 *England v. South Africa*

1. In Edgbaston's first Test match for fifteen years, in June 1924, South Africa were dismissed for 30 runs, as they had been at Port Elizabeth twenty-eight years earlier. Which two English bowlers bowled throughout the forty-eight minutes duration of the innings, taking 6–7 and 4–12 respectively, the latter, in the process, dismissing Manfred Susskind with his first ball in Test cricket?

2. Who scored a record 3,471 Test runs for South Africa in his forty-two appearances, all consecutive, failing to add to his total of eight centuries when being dismissed for 99 in his last match, against England at Port Elizabeth in March 1949?

3. Which brilliant South African fielder scored 127 at The Oval in August 1965, the only century of the final official Test match between England and South Africa?

4. Which two bowlers, county team-mates, claimed fifteen South African wickets between them in this same game, the one appearing in his seventieth and final Test match and taking 7 wickets to bring his Test aggregate to 252, and the other, on his début, capturing the first 8 of his eventual 71-wicket haul in Test cricket?

5. Which England player scored 148* against South Africa at Kingsmead, Durban, in December 1964, becoming in the process the first cricketer of any nationality to score a Test hundred in all of the then seven Test-playing countries?

6. Who, in his fifty-first and final Test match, conceded 61 runs in 10 overs at Old Trafford in July 1955, as South Africa reached a target of 145 in 135 minutes with nine balls to spare?

7. Which England batsman ended a sequence of low scores, by accumulating 219 in the second innings of the 'Timeless Test' at Durban in March 1939, though this was not good enough to retain his place for the following home series against the West Indies?

8. Who was the forty-two-year-old South African, the elder of two brothers playing in the Test, who scored 236 at Headingley in July 1951, the highest score by a South African against England?

9. Who was the twenty-one-year-old, making his Test début, who made 138 for England in the above match, the first Test début century in this country since 1896?

10. Who was the South African slow left-arm bowler who conceded only 10 runs in the course of twenty overs at Trent Bridge on his Test début in 1947, starting with eight consecutive maidens to Bill Edrich and Denis Compton, then in the middle of their famous run-scoring spree?

73 *Warwickshire*

1. Who scored his maiden first-class century for Warwickshire against Yorkshire at Edgbaston in August 1985, being frustratingly run out for 199?

2. Who scored 254, the highest innings for Warwickshire for nearly seventy years, when partnering Alvin Kallicharran in a Championship record fourth-wicket stand of 470, against Lancashire at Southport in 1982?

3. Who was the Warwickshire batsman who scored a record 17 sixes in the match against Lancashire at Blackpool in 1959, 10 in his first innings of 155 and 7 in his second innings 125?

4. Which former Warwickshire and England bowler scored only 1,544 runs in his 570 games for the county, but took 2,201 wickets, comfortably a Warwickshire record?

5. Who in 1962 became the first Warwickshire player since 1914 to achieve the 'double' of 1,000 runs and 100 wickets in a season for the county?

6. Whose fifty-nine-year-old record of 33,862 runs for Warwickshire did Dennis Amiss surpass in the course of the Britannic Assurance County Championship match against Glamorgan at Edgbaston in April 1987?

7. Which New Zealander failed to make his country's touring party to England in 1949, and indeed was never to play in a Test for New Zealand, but took 113 wickets for Warwickshire in that season – including 6–96 in an innings against the tourists – eventually finishing up with 695 wickets in his ten-year career with the county?

8. Who was the Warwickshire wicket-keeper who recorded 635 dismissals for the county between 1894 and 1911, in a career that was also to see him make thirty-five Test appearances for England between 1896 and 1909?

9. Who was the legendary all-rounder who led the county to their first Championship in 1911, achieving the 'double' in that year and again in 1914, when he also scored 305* against Worcestershire at Dudley, still the only triple century innings by a Warwickshire player?

10. Which bowler, who toured Australia with MCC in both 1920–21 and 1924–25, took all 10 wickets in an innings at Edgbaston in 1923, the first person to perform the feat for Warwickshire and the only man to do so against Yorkshire in the County Championship?

74 Test match bowling miscellany

1. Who took 85 Test wickets in 1981, a record total for a calendar year?

2. Who, playing against England at Madras in January 1964, conceded only five singles in thirty-two overs, during which he bowled 131 balls without a run being scored?

3. Who, at Headingley in 1983, took 10 England wickets, his best Test match haul, helping New Zealand to a first win on English soil in their twenty-ninth Test in this country?

4. Who, between 1925 and 1936, raced to 200 Test wickets in just thirty-six matches, the fewest needed to achieve this target to date?

5. Which fast bowler in November 1983, playing in only his second Test match, took 11-Pakistani wickets for 118 runs, a record match analysis for a Perth Test match, helping Australia to an innings victory?

6. Who in November 1983 took 9–83 in West Indies' second innings total of 201, but was unable to prevent the tourists' 138-run victory in Ahmedabad's inaugural Test?

7. Who achieved match figures of 11–83 for England against Pakistan at Karachi in March 1984, taking his wicket haul to 32 in his first four Test matches, a new English record?

8. Who was the nineteen-year-old leg-spinner who took 6 English wickets in each innings of the First Test at Bombay in 1984–85, so helping to end India's run of thirty-one Tests without a victory?

9. Which nineteen-year-old Australian fast bowler, over the 1985 New Year period, captured 10 West Indian wickets in his first two Test Matches, his victims being confined to the seven specialist batsmen, all of whom he dismissed at least once?

10. Who was the eighteen-year-old Pakistan fast bowler who, in February 1985 at Dunedin, playing in his second Test, captured 5 New Zealand wickets in each innings of the match?

75 *Christian names*

A further selection of post-war England Test cricketers to be identified from their middle names and potted Test career records:

	Middle name	Number of Tests	Year of first Test	Year of last Test	Runs	Wickets	Catches
1.	Barnard	4	1936	1947	47	–	1
2.	Benbow	11	1947	1952	881	2	6
3.	Cathie	3	1948	1949	157	–	5
4.	Dransfield	20	1938	1950	812	21	14
5.	Fletcher	3	1948	1948	20	4	–
6.	Holmes	17	1954	1959	230	76	4
7.	Middleton	46	1972	1981	845	143	22
8.	Parson	34	1938	1951	289	108	10
9.	Thompson	7	1951	1955	354	–	10 & 2 st.
10.	Thornton	8	1978	1978	481	–	4

76 Benson and Hedges Cup

1. Who won the Gold Award in the 1987 Benson and Hedges Cup Final for his match-winning innings of 75,* which secured his county's first Benson and Hedges title?

2. Which county thought they had ensured their passage to the quarter-finals of the 1979 Benson and Hedges Cup by declaring their innings closed after one over against Worcestershire, thereby allowing their opponents to win, but denying them the opportunity to improve their wicket-taking rate and go to the top of the Group table?

3. Who won the Man of the Match award in the 1984 Benson and Hedges Cup Final although he was dismissed without scoring and did not bowl?

4. Who made 132* in his team's total of 197–3 in the 1981 Benson and Hedges Cup Final?

5. Who bowled eleven overs for 16 against Kent in the 1985 Benson and Hedges Cup Final, having a major bearing on his team's victory by a margin of 2 runs when the allotted overs were completed?

6. Who beat Lancashire by 3 runs in a zonal match in the 1986 Benson and Hedges Cup, for a first victory in twenty-six games in the competition?

7. Which pair scored 211 to beat Warwickshire in a Benson and Hedges Cup match in May 1987, the highest undefeated opening partnership in the history of the competition?

8. Which county lost their last five wickets for 7 runs to lose the 1983 Benson and Hedges Cup Final to Middlesex by just 4 runs?

9. Who scored 92 in the 1981 Benson and Hedges Cup Final, the highest individual innings by a member of the losing side in the final of the competition?

10. Who took a hat-trick in the 1974 Benson and Hedges Cup Final and finished with figures of 4 for 10, but could not prevent Surrey beating Leicestershire by 27 runs?

77 Worcestershire

1. Which infrequent batsman was sent in as Worcestershire's 'night-watchman' when the score was 0–1 v. Warwickshire in July 1987, and proceeded to bat throughout the innings, finishing with 120* out of 285, his maiden first-class century?

2. Who was the twenty-year-old Worcestershire batsman who scored over 2,000 runs in the 1986 season, the youngest ever player to achieve the feat?

3. Who took over 100 wickets for Worcestershire in 1985, and repeated the feat in 1987, on both occasions being the only bowler in the County Championship to reach the three figure target?

4. Who ended an illustrious fifteen-year career with Worcestershire in 1982, scoring five centuries in just sixteen innings, including 311* in a day against Warwickshire, a performance made more memorable because it was his 100th century in first-class cricket?

5. Who made a record 589 appearances for Worcestershire, scoring a record 33,490 runs in the process, and had the added distinction of leading the county to Championship success in both 1964 and 1965?

6. Four Worcestershire players took 100 wickets for the county in the 1961 season: Len Coldwell, Jack Flavell, Norman Gifford and which other player, who was performing the feat for the only time and coupled his 101 wickets with 1,808 runs, being the only player from the county to perform the 'double' in county matches alone since the Second World War?

7. Which Worcestershire leg-break and googly bowler achieved the rare feat of taking two hat-tricks in the same match, one in each innings, against Surrey at Worcester in 1949?

8. Who was the former Yorkshire wicket-keeper who recorded 1,015 dismissals for Worcestershire in 402 appearances between 1956 and 1970, and in 1964 was the last wicket-keeper to achieve 100 victims in a County Championship season?

9. Who was the left-hand batsman and occasional bowler, capped once by England, in 1957, who held 412 catches for Worcestershire in 371 matches between 1952 and 1967?

10. Who was the future Test match umpire who kept wicket for Worcestershire in 110 matches between 1935 and 1946, claiming 232 career dismissals?

78 *England v. Australia – Test miscellany*

1. Who was the England captain, born in Sydney, Australia, who had the misfortune to lose the 1936–37 Ashes series after the first two Tests had been won?

2. Which pair, batting down the order to take advantage of a Melbourne wicket that had lost its 'devil', shared a sixth-wicket partnership of 346 in January 1937, still a Test record for this wicket?

3. Who, playing in his last Test match, scored 266 at The Oval in 1934, sharing with Don Bradman a second-wicket partnership of 451 which still stands as a Test record for any wicket, though it was equalled in 1983?

4. Who, playing for Australia against England at Adelaide in January 1933, carried his bat for 73* out of a total of 193, having previously achieved the same feat in December 1928 at Brisbane, scoring 30* in Australia's total of 66?

5. Who came in as a night-watchman for England in the final Test at Sydney in February 1933 and stayed to score 98, his highest score in Test cricket and only four runs short of his career best?

6. Who made his Test match début for England in the First Test of the 1932–33 'Bodyline' series and scored 102, one of England's three centuries in a First innings total of 524?

7. Who was the highly successful England captain who made his only Test century when scoring 121 in England's second innings against Australia at Lord's in June and July 1930?

8. When the twenty-year-old Don Bradman made his Test début at Brisbane in November 1928, who was the forty-five-year-old left-arm spinner, also making a first appearance for Australia, and, unlike Bradman, retained his place for the following Test.

9. Which England bowler took 6–32 and 2–30 in the First Test at Brisbane in 1928–29, but thereafter lost form and had figures of 10 wickets for 662 runs in the remaining four Tests?

10. Who made his début for Australia at the age of 19 years and 152 days, at Adelaide in February 1929, scoring 164 against England in Australia's first innings, though his career was to be tragically curtailed when he died of tuberculosis at just 23 years of age?

79 Cricket records

1. Who in 1981 equalled a world record when he caught out eleven Derbyshire batsmen in one first-class match?

2. Who scored a century in thirty-five minutes for Lancashire against Leicestershire at Old Trafford in September 1983?

3. Which county won a Championship match in 1956 without losing a wicket?

4. Against which county did the 1948 Australian touring team score 721 runs in one day?

5. Who was the leading English batsman in the first-class averages in every season between 1933 and 1946?

6. Who achieved a record 64 stumpings in 1932, but only 36 catches, so recording exactly 100 dismissals during the season?

7. Which twice-capped wicket-keeper did not concede a bye while 2,132 runs were scored against his county during 1965?

8. Which county scored 543–4 against Sussex in 1920, with the first four batsmen all scoring centuries, and scored 642–3 against Hampshire in 1923, with the first four in the batting order again all reaching treble figures?

9. Which county was dismissed for 15 runs by Warwickshire in 1922, and following on scored 521, winning the match by 155 runs?

10. Which county was dismissed by Yorkshire in 1908 for a match aggregate of 42 runs, 27 in the first innings and 15 in the second?

80 Gillette Cup/NatWest Trophy finals – The players

1. Which opening batsman appeared in two Gillette Cup finals, on the losing side in 1967 but scoring 53 nine years later as Northamptonshire defeated holders Lancashire by four wickets?

2. Which medium-pace bowler, now a county secretary, appeared in both of Northamptonshire's losing sixty-over finals in 1979 and 1981, having previously appeared for another losing side in 1975?

3. Which middle-order batsman and under-rated bowler won a Gillette Cup winners' medal for one county prior to receiving another winners' medal in the inaugural NatWest Trophy final – against his former county?

4. Which left-arm bowler played in the Kent side which lost to Lancashire in the 1971 Gillette Cup Final, but five years later got the better of Lancashire as a Northamptonshire player?

5. Which two batsmen were the only players to appear in all Middlesex's three Gillette Cup final appearances between 1975 and 1980, as well as their first appearance, in 1984, in a NatWest Trophy final?

6. Which England left-arm opening bowler, while playing for two different counties, was a losing Gillette Cup finalist in both 1967 and 1969?

7. Who was the defeated captain in the last Gillette Cup final in 1980, returning two years later as a winner in the newly constituted NatWest Trophy final, though he had in fact won a Gillette Cup winners' medal nine years earlier with Gloucestershire?

8. Who in 1964 and 1966 played in both of Warwickshire's first two Gillette Cup finals, taking 3–16 as they redeemed their earlier defeat in 1966, and eleven years later was to reappear in the final as a Glamorgan player?

9. Who was the only man playing for Derbyshire when they won the inaugural NatWest Trophy final in 1981 who had played in their Gillette Cup final defeat in 1969 at the hands of Yorkshire?

10. Who played in all of Lancashire's six Gillette Cup final appearances between 1970 and 1976, and has since played in a NatWest Trophy final for another county?

81 *Yorkshire*

1. Who was the nineteen-year-old who scored 122 on his début for Yorkshire in August 1983 against Nottinghamshire at Bradford?

2. Who, at 16 years and 2½ months, became Yorkshire's youngest ever Championship player in September 1981, and the following season, still not seventeen, performed an 'all bowled' hat-trick in a John Player League match at Derby? When he took his next hat-trick – also against Derbyshire – in July 1985 he was still, at the age of twenty, the youngest player to take a hat-trick for the county.

3. Who shared an opening partnership of 351 with Geoff Boycott for Yorkshire against Worcestershire at Worcester in June 1985?

4. Who made 462 appearances for Yorkshire between 1951 and 1968, returning as captain in the middle of the 1982 season at fifty years of age?

5. Which bowler in 1969 was the last Yorkshire player to take over 100 wickets in a first-class season?

6. Who made 491 consecutive appearances for Yorkshire between 1955 and 1969, retiring at the age of thirty-three without ever having missed a match?

7. Which great Yorkshire bowler achieved the most outstanding innings performance in county cricket, taking 10 wickets for 10 runs from 19 overs and 4 balls, against Nottinghamshire at Headingley in July 1932?

8. Which legendary Yorkshireman made 881 appearances for the county, over 100 more than anyone else has made for any county, during which period he scored 31,156 runs and took 3,608 wickets, achieving the 'double' a record twelve times?

9. Which two Yorkshire cricketers were the respective leaders of the domestic batting and bowling averages at the end of the 1930 season?

10. Who was the aristocrat who captained Yorkshire from 1883 to 1910, and served as President of the County Cricket Club from 1898 until his death in 1938, though remarkably, in view of Yorkshire's tradition, he was not born in the county but hailed from neighbouring Lincolnshire?

82 *Test batting – General*

1. Which batsman scored Sri Lanka's first century in official Tests, 157 against Pakistan at Faisalabad in March 1982, and surpassed this in August 1984 when his 190 in 636 minutes became the longest ever Test century at Lord's?

2. Which practising journalist, later to pen some of the most authoritative accounts of Ashes Test series, set a new world record in 1936 when he became the first player to score centuries in four consecutive Test innings, his attempt to make it five failing rather ignominiously when he was bowled first ball by England's Bill Voce?

3. Which Indian batsman scored 200* against New Zealand at Bombay in March 1965, sharing in a record sixth-wicket stand for his country of 193, unbroken, with Hanumant Singh – a record that still exists – and at Bridgetown in April 1971 scored 150 and shared a record seventh-wicket partnership of 186 with Eddie Solkar which stood until December 1984?

4. Which post-war Indian Test player, playing against New Zealand in Hyderabad in November 1955, scored his country's first ever Test double century, and was to record twelve Test centuries in all but never one against Australia?

5. Who, playing against Pakistan in December 1983, was the last batsman to exceed 250 runs in a Test innings, before Javed Miandad scored 260 for Pakistan in August 1987?

6. Who scored 123 runs before lunch on the third morning of the 1935 Oval Test Match against South Africa, when progressing from 25* to 148*?

7. Which West Indian, at Perth in December 1975, reached a Test hundred in 116 minutes off just seventy-one balls on the way to a score of 169?

8. Who scored 336* in 318 minutes for England against New Zealand at Auckland in April 1933, scoring his third hundred in only forty-seven minutes in an innings which included a Test record of 10 sixes?

9. Which player, on his Test début in April 1987 against New Zealand at Colombo, became the first Sri Lankan to score a Test double century, and only the third person of any nationality to do so in his first Test?

10. When Bill Lawry was dropped as captain and opening batsman for the Seventh Test against England in February 1971, who was his fellow Victorian, also left-handed, who replaced him to make his only Test appearance at the age of thirty-five, two years older than Lawry?

83 *Domestic cricket abroad*

1. Which player in December 1987 scored 294 for Orange Free State against Eastern Province, surpassing a twenty-eight-year-old State record, and sharing in a fifth-wicket partnership of 355 with Joubert Strydom, a new South African domestic record previously held by Graeme Pollock and Lorrie Wilmot since 1975–76?

2. Who was the South African bowler who took all 10 wickets in an innings for Western Province against Orange Free State at Newlands in December 1987?

3. Who scored the fastest recorded first-class century in terms of balls received, reaching 102 off thirty-four balls in forty-three minutes, when captaining South Australia against Victoria at the Adelaide Oval in October 1982?

4. Which inappropriately named Indian cricketer bowled thirty-nine overs in an innings on his Test début in October 1983, taking 2–65 against Pakistan at Nagpur, a fairly mundane spell of bowling compared with his ninety-four overs in an innings for Karnataka in the 1981–82 Ranji Trophy Final when he took 1–179 against Delhi?

5. Which wicket-keeper, playing against South Australia in January 1977, achieved the unique double of scoring a century and taking ten catches in the same match?

6. Which two players in March 1987 shared an unbroken partnership of 462 for the fourth wicket for South Australia against Tasmania, beating an Australian record for any wicket, previously set in 1923–24 by Bill Ponsford and Edgar Mayne?

7. Prior to the above match, who was the last player to score a triple century in Australian domestic cricket?

8. Which famous English Test player scored 249* for Holkar in the 1945 Ranji Trophy Final, yet his side lost by 374 runs to Bombay, for whom Vijay Merchant scored 278?

9. Which twenty-seven-year-old Victoria and Australian Test player became, in December 1927, the only man to score 1,000 runs in a month during a non-English season, scoring 1,146 in five innings at an average of 229.20?

10. Who, just one month after his only Test appearance, took 10–61 for Queensland against Victoria at Melbourne in January 1966, the first bowler to take all 10 wickets in an innings of a Sheffield Shield match since Tom Wall for South Australia, thirty-three years earlier?

84 *The Prudential World Cup*

1. Who scored the first century in a Prudential World Cup match when hitting 137 for England against India in the opening game of the inaugural tournament in 1975?

2. Who scored 171* against East Africa and 114* against India in 1975, the only player to score two centuries in the inaugural World Cup competition?

3. Who scored a century before lunch for Australia in the 1975 Prudential World Cup tournament, their only three-figure innings in the inaugural competition?

4. Who took 6 wickets for 14 runs when Australia bowled England out for 93 in the semi-final of the 1975 Prudential World Cup and, playing against the West Indies in the final, followed it up with 5–48?

5. Who scored 102 for the West Indies in the 1975 Prudential World Cup Final, an innings that ultimately decided the match as his team won by a mere 17 runs, while he himself took the Man of the Match award?

6. Who was the England captain in the 1975 Prudential World Cup tournament?

7. Which player, in the course of an innings of 55, batted eleven successive overs without scoring a run in the inaugural World Cup final in 1975?

8. Which country, a qualifier from the International Cricket Conference Trophy tournament, were dismissed for only 45 runs against England in the 1979 Prudential World Cup?

9. Who outscored Vivian Richards when making 86 in a fifth-wicket partnership of 139 in twenty-one overs for the West Indies against England in the 1979 Prudential World Cup Final?

10. Who took 5 wickets in eleven balls as England collapsed from 183–2 to 194 all out in the 1979 Prudential World Cup Final?

85 *County grounds*

1. Which ground, used for the World Cup in 1983, was the venue the last time that a County Championship match was started and finished on the same day, the 15 June 1960?

2. Which county plays on May's Bounty ground and in 1986 made 401–5 declared, the highest innings total in eighty years of first-class cricket at the venue?

3. On which English ground did Don Bradman score 807 runs in four innings for an average of 201.75?

4. Which county plays occasional matches at the Griff and Coton Ground?

5. Which first-class county has played Championship cricket at Luton?

6. On which ground did Archie MacLaren make the highest individual score in a County Championship match?

7. On which ground did Tony Lock capture all 10 Kent wickets in one innings in 1956?

8. On which ground, during the 1983 Prudential World Cup, did Pakistan and Sri Lanka achieve the then highest innings total and match aggregate in one-day international cricket?

9. On which ground in 1932 did Percy Holmes and Herbert Sutcliffe share a County Championship record first-wicket partnership of 555 runs?

10. On which ground did Kent's Arthur Fagg uniquely score a double century in each innings of a County Championship match against Essex in 1938?

86 *England v. Australia*

1. Which two players, at Adelaide in February 1947, were respectively the last Englishman and the last Australian to score a century in each innings of an Ashes Test?

2. Which thirty-year-old New South Wales off-spinner, playing in only his seventh first-class match, became in January 1987 the first Australian to take 6 wickets in an innings on his Test début since Rodney Hogg in 1978, when he finished with figures of 6–78 in Australia's 55-run win over England at Sydney?

3. Who played in twenty Test matches for England against Australia between March 1929 and August 1938, scoring 1,705 runs at an average of 56.83, but averaged only 34.16 in his other twenty-one Tests against India, South Africa and the West Indies?

4. Who opened the England innings in all five Tests against Australia in 1961, scoring a century in the first and the last matches of his only series against the 'old enemy'?

5. Who played for Australia in a record fifteen different series against England between 1876 and 1895?

6. Who was the only cricketer to have played for Australia against England, and for England against Australia?

7. Who scored 99, 98 and 97 in successive Test innings against England in January 1902?

8. Who is the only Australian to take 9 English wickets in an innings?

9. Who made his Test début against Australia at Lord's in August 1975 at thirty-three years of age, and in three matches made 365 runs at an average of 60.83, with a highest score of 92 and a lowest of 39?

10. Who was the nineteen-year-old who scored 155 against England on his Test début in December 1965 at Woolloongabba, Brisbane?

87 Career statistics – Batsmen

1. Which batsman, in a career that lasted from 1957 to 1983, scored 36,049 first-class runs, a record for a non-Englishman?

2. Which batsman, in a career that lasted from 1945 to 1972, held the original record for a non-Englishman of 35,725 first-class runs, and also scored 30,303 runs in county cricket after the end of his Test career, a record in Championship cricket?

3. Which player in 1928 scored a record, 2,843 runs in a County Championship season and, in a career lasting from 1906 to 1936, also set Championship records of 46,268 runs and 132 centuries?

4. Who is the only batsman to score 6,000 runs in Test cricket before reaching the age of thirty?

5. Who scored 47,793 runs in 1,223 first-class innings between 1948 and 1971, a post-war record until overtaken by Geoffrey Boycott in 1986?

6. Who was the seventh and most recent batsman to exceed 50,000 runs in a first-class career?

7. Who holds the distinction of being the only cricketer to score over 10,000 runs in a completed career without scoring a century, totalling 10,342 in 812 innings between 1946 and 1970, with a highest score of 89?

8. Which post-war batsman retired with a career average of 56.83, to surpass Wally Hammond's record of 56.10 for a batsman scoring more than 30,000 runs?

9. Who, between 1906 and 1938, played a record 1,530 innings, accumulating 58,959 runs which included 145 centuries?

10. Who, in twenty-three seasons between 1949 and 1971, scored 30,225 runs in 601 matches for Sussex, which included 423 consecutive County Championship appearances between August 1954 and July 1969? He never played for England, but did field as a substitute at Port-of-Spain in March 1954 and caught Everton Weekes off the bowling of Fred Trueman.

88 *Benson and Hedges Cup finals– The players*

1. Who played for the losing side, Worcestershire, in both the 1973 and 1976 Benson and Hedges Cup finals against Kent but, having returned to the county of his birth, took a winners' medal in the final against Warwickshire in 1984?

2. Which two brothers, both opening batsmen, played for different counties in Benson and Hedges Cup finals, the elder taking a runners-up medal in 1979, but the younger a winners' in 1985?

3. Who scored 0 for Kent in the 1977 Benson and Hedges Cup Final and was slightly more successful when scoring 6 for Surrey in 1981, though his teams' fortunes tended to mirror his own performances and he was left with two losers' medals?

4. Which England international is the only player to have appeared for more than one county in Benson and Hedges Cup finals and has yet to play on the losing side, his three winners' medals coming between 1978 and 1986?

5. Who appeared for Worcestershire in their losing Benson and Hedges Cup final in 1973 against Kent but, having moved counties, he achieved figures of 3–9 in the defeat of Kent in the 1977 final?

6. Which two brothers both won runners-up medals in the 1986 Benson and Hedges Cup Final in spite of the younger's valiant 58 in a two-run defeat?

7. Who won a runners-up medal with Worcestershire in 1973 but, having moved to Northamptonshire, was in the team which defeated holders Essex in the 1980 Benson and Hedges Cup Final?

8. Which veteran won a runners-up medal in the 1984 Benson and Hedges Cup Final, having previously captained another county to defeat in the final?

9. Which bowler took 0–23 in his eleven overs as his county lost to Kent by 6 wickets in the 1978 Benson and Hedges Cup Final, and four years later was also to receive a runners-up medal, taking the only wicket as his new county were thrashed by Somerset, losing by 9 wickets?

10. Who took his third Benson and Hedges Cup winners' medal in 1979, having previously played in Kent's victorious teams in 1973 and 1976, and was to experience defeat in the final only when returning with his new team the following season?

89 *Around the counties*

1. Who in 1951 set a world record when making 6 stumpings in an innings, achieving the feat against Scotland at Broughty Ferry?

2. Who was the thirty-eight-year-old Worcestershire all-rounder who in 1947 scored 1,510 runs and took 164 wickets, the only man since the Second World War to achieve the 'double' of 1,500 runs and 150 wickets in an English first-class season?

3. Who bowled over 250 no-balls for Glamorgan in the course of the 1983 County Championship?

4. Who in 1985 became the first overseas player to be capped by three different counties?

5. Who made the highest first-class score by an Englishman in the month of April when registering 248 for Hampshire against Cambridge University in 1984?

6. Who was the Northamptonshire medium-pace bowler who took 348 wickets for the county but, conversely, scored only 207 runs, in addition to possessing the unenviable record of having failed to get off the mark in ten consecutive innings?

7. Who were the young Surrey representatives who scored 101* and 117* respectively against Cambridge University in 1984, the first occasion on which two team-mates have both scored centuries on their first-class débuts in the same match?

8. Who, in his 618th innings, scored his maiden first-class century at Hastings in 1984, a match that also became memorable for producing the first 'tie' in the County Championship for ten years?

9. Which county in 1984 became the first to win the Championship and the Sunday League titles in the same season?

10. Who had match figures of 11–99 against Yorkshire in 1984, a personal analysis not quite equalling his 11–46 *for* Yorkshire in 1969?

90 *Wicket-keepers in Test cricket*

1. Which Central Districts wicket-keeper in March 1987 became the first man to record 100 dismissals in Test cricket for New Zealand?

2. Who were England's four wicket-keepers in the First Test Match against New Zealand at Lord's in July 1986?

3. Which wicket-keeper scored 69 and 182, as well as holding 6 catches in an innings, against Australia at Johannesburg in December 1966, going on to score 606 runs in the series, a record by a wicket-keeper?

4. Which England wicket-keeper was the first former professional player to be elected a Test selector?

5. Who in 1925 stumped four of England's first seven batsmen in the same innings in the Fourth Test at Melbourne, ending his Test career ten years later as the only wicket-keeper to achieve 50 stumpings in Test cricket?

6. Which Australian wicket-keeper, making his Test début in December 1957 against South Africa at Johannesburg, became the first man to take 6 catches in an innings of a Test match?

7. Which Australian wicket-keeper, playing against the West Indies at Brisbane in November 1951, caught 3 and stumped 4 on his Test début?

8. Which forty-seven-year-old conceded 37 byes when deputising for Leslie Ames in the second innings of the Oval Test against Australia in 1934, in what proved to be his final Test match?

9. Which future New Zealand captain took the field as substitute wicket-keeper in the final session of the Second Test Match against Pakistan at Lahore in April 1965, and stumped Pakistan's Pervez Sajjad, only the second time in the history of Test cricket that a replacement wicket-keeper has performed a stumping?

10. Which Surrey and England wicket-keeper became, in March 1914, the first to attain 20 or more dismissals in a Test series when catching 15 and stumping 6 on the tour of South Africa?

91 *England v. Australia*

1. Don Bradman took 2 Test wickets in his career, both at Adelaide, trapping West Indies wicket-keeper, Ivan Barrow, leg before wicket in December 1930, before bowling which England batsman two years later in the infamous 'Bodyline' Test?

2. The first occasion on which a bowler was to take 30 or more wickets in a Test series was in 1894–95 when George Giffin's 34 for Australia at 24.12 was almost matched by which Surrey and England bowler's 32 at 26.53?

3. Which player scored 11 in England's first innings in the 1981 Old Trafford Test, before becoming Dennis Lillee's 150th wicket in Ashes Tests, and in the second innings, after Ian Botham's heroics, recorded his fortieth 'not out' in Test matches, beating a record previously shared by Lance Gibbs and Bhagwat Chandrasekhar?

4. Which bowler, with a match analysis of 11–134 at Brisbane in November 1982, was the last Australian to take 10 or more wickets in an Ashes Test?

5. Which Australian batsman was dismissed eighteen times by Alec Bedser in Test matches, the most times that one particular batsman has been dismissed by any one bowler?

6. Which player was voted Man of the Match on his Test début for Australia against England at Brisbane in November 1982?

7. Who, when taking 8–141 in August 1985, became the first Australian to take 8 wickets in an innings of an Old Trafford Test since Frank Laver's 8–31, still Australia's best analysis in England, in July 1909?

8. Following Ken Barrington's 256 at Old Trafford in July 1964, who was the next England batsman to score a double century in an Ashes Test?

9. Which Yorkshire bowler made his Test début at Lords against Australia in 1948, took 2–90 and 1–82 in the match, and was never again selected?

10. Who scored 905 runs in an Ashes series in 1928–29, a record superseded by Don Bradman's 974 in 1930, although it still stands as the English record for any series?

92 Hat-tricks

1. Who was the substitute who held the catch that gave Eddie Barlow his hat-trick for the Rest of the World against England at Headingley in July 1970?

2. Which all-rounder, as well as scoring 55 and 85 for the MCC against the 1975 Australians, also performed the hat-trick in the match, the first to do so against the Australian tourists since Middlesex's Henry Enthoven in 1934, and by coincidence he performed the feat on the day of Enthoven's funeral?

3. Which bowler, who played in 404 matches for his county between 1965 and 1984, taking 1,016 wickets, took the only hat-trick of his career in a 'Test Trial' at Hove in 1973, but was never to play for England?

4. Which leg-break bowler, playing for Australia against South Africa at Old Trafford in the Triangular Tournament of 1912, is the only man to take a hat-trick in each innings of a Test match, these being his only 6 wickets in the match?

5. Who is the Calcutta-born bowler who played nine Tests for South Africa in 1935 and 1936 and played eight times for Worcestershire in 1938, but whose main claim to fame is that, as a Western Province player in the early 1930s, he is the only man to have twice taken 4 wickets in four balls?

6. Who took the second hat-trick of his career, some sixteen years after his first, when dismissing Kent's first three batsmen – Neil Taylor, Derek Aslett and Chris Tavaré – at Canterbury in June 1987?

7. Who in March 1904 took his second Test match hat-trick, at Melbourne on his final appearance for Australia, when he claimed the last 7 England wickets at a personal cost of 28 runs?

8. Who in 1960 took the first hat-trick for South Africa, and also the first at Lord's in a Test match, but had his pleasure at this achievement tempered by being no-balled eleven times for throwing and never played Test cricket again?

9. Who scored 100 and took a hat-trick against Essex in 1972, and repeated this achievement against Leicestershire in 1979?

10. Who took 4 wickets in five balls, including a hat-trick, for England against New Zealand at Lancaster Park, Christchurch, in January 1930, his first victims on his Test match début?

93 *County Championship – Best bowling*

1. Three bowlers took 10 wickets in an innings in the 1956 first-class season: Jim Laker twice against the Australians, his county compatriot, Tony Lock, against Kent, and which former Yorkshire spinner, who recorded figures of 10–66 for Nottinghamshire v. Gloucestershire at Stroud?

2. Which spin bowler took all 10 Warwickshire wickets in an innings in May 1931, two months prior to his England début, and all 10 Nottinghamshire wickets in an innings in July 1932?

3. Which overseas fast bowler, in his first County Championship season in 1985, took 8–40 against Yorkshire, including 4 wickets in five balls?

4. Which Test captain achieved a career-best 8–34 when Middlesex were routed for 70 at Lord's in May 1986?

5. Who was the future England bowler who achieved a career-best return of 13–86 against Essex at Southend in July 1986?

6. Which Leicestershire cricketer scored 53*, batting at number ten, against Glamorgan in August 1971, and then captured 7 wickets for 8 runs as the Welshmen collapsed to 24 all out, his match return being 11–37?

7. Who claimed 7 Gloucestershire wickets in each innings of a County Championship match at Harrogate in September 1967, conceding only six runs from his thirteen overs in Gloucestershire's second innings?

8. Who had match figures of 9–11 and 8–56 when Kent dismissed Sussex for 47 and 126, at Hove in 1922?

9. Who captured 8 wickets in both innings for match figures of 16–83, Nottinghamshire's best post-war analysis, as his county beat Essex by an innings and 88 runs in 1954?

10. Who plundered 17 wickets in one day in 1907, taking 10–30 and 7–18 for Kent against Northamptonshire?

94 *Australian cricket*

1. Which prolific Victoria State batsman scored 1,580 runs at an average of 121·54 in his first nine first-class matches and, at a later stage in his career, scored eleven centuries in eighteen innings on Australian soil?

2. Which New Zealand born bowler took 513 wickets in seventy-nine Sheffield Shield matches between 1918 and 1941, nearly 200 more than anyone else has ever achieved?

3. Which famous Australian leg-break and googly bowler conceded a record 362 runs in an innings, in the 1926–27 Australian season?

4. Which Australian Test wicket-keeper claimed 12 dismissals in a match for Queensland against New South Wales in 1938–39, to equal the seventy-year-old world record of Edward Pooley?

5. Who scored 1,538 runs for South Australia in 1970–71, at an average of 109.86, including an innings of 356 against Western Australia at Perth, 325 of which came in one day?

6. Which man, who played in six Tests for Australia between 1968 and 1972, five of them in England, captained Western Australia for five seasons during the 1970s, leading them to the Sheffield Shield title on four occasions?

7. Which state, still seeking its first Sheffield Shield title, lost to New South Wales by just one wicket in the 1984–85 final?

8. Which veteran English off-break bowler played twenty matches for Tasmania between 1972 and 1979?

9. Who was the highly successful Australian Test bowler who, in 1887–8, took 106 wickets for New South Wales, remaining, a full century later, the only bowler to record 100 wickets in an Australian season?

10. Don Bradman's Sheffield Shield career was divided almost equally between two states – he played for his native New South Wales from 1927 until 1934, but which state did he represent from 1935 until 1949?

95 Miscellaneous tours

1. Which three Englishmen – from Derbyshire, Worcestershire and Yorkshire respectively – toured Australia with the Rest of the World team in 1971–72?

2. Which young Lancastrian captained England Young Cricketers on their tour to Sri Lanka in early 1987?

3. Which former England captain was manager of the Rest of the World team on their 1970 tour of England?

4. Which seventeen-year-old scored 118 and 120* for the England Young Cricketers in their Third Test Match against Sri Lanka Young Cricketers in February 1987, and within two months was making his first-class début, for Middlesex against Yorkshire?

5. Which country was captained by Henry Robinson, a former Oxford Blue, on an eighteen-match unofficial tour of England in 1954, which included four games against first-class county sides?

6. Which future Test cricketer sprang to prominence on an England Young Cricketers tour of the West Indies in 1976–77 when he topped the batting averages as well as taking most wickets?

7. Which Test player, representing an International XI against a West Indies XI at Kingston in September 1982, was the last Englishman to take all 10 wickets in an innings of a first-class match, his 175 runs conceded (in 49.3 overs) being the most by any bowler achieving the feat?

8. Which Sussex medium-pace bowler, touring India and Ceylon with the MCC in 1926–27, took 116 wickets in a non-English season – a record which still stands?

9. Which player in February 1987 scored 135 and 105 * in an unofficial Test match against the country of his birth?

10. Which player, who made six double centuries in a five-year spell in county cricket between 1978 and 1982, scored 173 and 105* for South Africa against the 'rebel' Australians in the second unofficial Test at Cape Town in January 1987?

96 One-day internationals

1. Who, making his return to the England team after three years absence, scored two successive centuries in Texaco Trophy matches against Australia in June 1985?

2. Who saved his country after an early collapse with an innings of 189*, the highest in international one-day cricket, at Old Trafford in 1984?

3. Who scored 12* to share a last-wicket stand of 106 in the above match, the first three-figure partnership for the tenth wicket in one-day internationals?

4. Which country easily won the 1985 Benson and Hedges World Championship, held in Melbourne to celebrate the 150th anniversary of the founding of the state of Victoria?

5. Which two players shared a record unbeaten partnership of 224 when Australia beat Sri Lanka by an unprecedented margin of 232 runs in the Benson and Hedges World Series Cup in March 1985?

6. Who, without once being dismissed, scored 234 runs in four one-day international innings (including two separate centuries) for Pakistan against India in December 1982 and January 1983?

7. Who captained Australia in the first ever one-day international match, at Melbourne in January 1971, his only appearance in a game of this nature?

8. Who, at Old Trafford in August 1972, scored the first century in a one-day international?

9. Who, at The Oval in September 1973, became the first West Indian to score a century in a one-day International?

10. Which wicket-keeper scored his only century in international cricket, for New Zealand against Australia at Christchurch in March 1974?

97 Overseas players in the County Championship

1. For which county did Keith Miller play just one game, against Cambridge University in 1959, scoring a century and taking 2–35?

2. Which Australian opening bowler topped the English national bowling averages in 1979 with 19 wickets at 12.10, from three appearances for Lancashire?

3. Which Sydney-born left-hand batsman and right-arm bowler, who played 350 games for his county between 1957 and 1968, performed the only 'double' of his career in 1962, when scoring 1,915 runs at 36.83 and taking 112 wickets at 20.74, but did not make his first appearance in a Test match until 1974?

4. Which Sydney-born left-hand batsman scored 13,165 runs for Northamptonshire in the years 1950 to 1957, scoring over 2,000 runs in the successive seasons 1954 and 1955?

5. Which Australian opening batsman scored nearly 3,000 runs, in total, for Essex in 1971 and 1973, averaging over 38 runs per innings in each season?

6. Which county did the legendary Australian bowler Fred 'The Demon' Spofforth represent between 1889 and 1891, once taking 15 Yorkshire wickets for 81?

7. Who was the Charlton Athletic footballer who played Test cricket for South Africa, averaging over 32 against England in 1960, who also played 26 matches for Kent between 1951 and 1954 as deputy wicket-keeper to Godfrey Evans?

8. Who announced his retirement from Test cricket in 1987 after scoring over 3,000 runs, including nine centuries, in sixty Test matches for the West Indies, but achieved a best score of only 93* in forty-two matches for Middlesex between 1973 and 1976?

9. Which county did Michael Holding represent in seven matches in 1981 before joining Derbyshire in 1983 on a rather more permanent basis?

10. Which mighty hitting West Indian batsman and useful medium-pace bowler played sixteen matches for Glamorgan in 1977?

98 *Family connections*

1. William Cooper, born in Maidstone, Kent, played in two Tests for Australia in the 1880s, batting number eleven on each occasion, but who was his great-grandson, a far more accomplished batsman, who played in thirty-one Tests for Australia between 1967 and 1974, scoring 1,594 runs at an average of 33.91?

2. Who won the Man of the Match award for Kent in their 1982 Benson and Hedges zonal match against Surrey, emulating his father before him and becoming the first father and son combination to win Gold Awards in the competition?

3. Who was the grandfather of the Chappell brothers who himself played nineteen times for Australia, five times as captain, between 1924 and 1936, and at Durban in his last Test took 5 catches in an innings, a record for an outfielder unequalled for forty-one years?

4. Which 22-times capped Indian cricketer scored 265 in the 1980–81 Ranji Trophy Final, surpassing his 44-times-capped father's best performance in the final, 185 in 1936–37?

5. Imran Khan, Pakistan's captain, has two cousins who have also captained their country – Majid Khan and which other player who led the side on their tour of England in 1962?

6. Who were the father and son who between them played seventy-nine times for South Africa? The father, although scoring 72 on his début in 1902, had to wait until 1921, his sixty-fourth innings, for his first century, while the son scored nine Test centuries including the first double century against England by a South African, 208 at Trent Bridge in 1951.

7. Which player in February 1987 scored 101, his maiden Test century, thirty-two years after his father had scored the first of his twelve hundreds for his country?

8. In family terms, what was the connection between Pakistan's draw with New Zealand in Karachi in December 1984 and their innings defeat by India in Delhi in October 1952?

9. As well as his cricketing brother, David Steele also played alongside his cousin when coming into the Northamptonshire side in 1963. Who was this stalwart who played 317 games for the county between 1960 and 1972, scoring over 8,000 runs and taking over 800 wickets?

10. Who is the son of the NCA national coach who, playing for his father's former county, scored his maiden first-class century in May 1987, the first to be scored against the touring Pakistanis?

99 Test cricket – Mixed bag

1. Which former Test player became the first ever official substitute umpire to stand in a Test match when temporarily replacing the injured Dickie Bird in the First Test between England and Pakistan at Old Trafford in June 1987?

2. Who in February 1987 in the first ever Test to be played at Jaipur, represented his country 17 years and 111 days after his previous Test appearance, against New Zealand in Lahore?

3. Who refused to play for his country in Calcutta in February 1987, on account of abuse he had received there in a Test match some two years earlier?

4. Which England cricketer made his Test début in February 1971, did not play again until December 1977, but subsequently appeared in a further fifty-six Tests, though never against the West Indies?

5. When Dandeniyage 'D.S.' De Silva failed to make the Sri Lanka team in the First Test v. India in Colombo in August 1985, his country's thirteenth official Test match, who was left as Sri Lanka's only surviving player from their inaugural Test in February 1982, and in fact went on to make his maiden Test century in the match?

6. Which Yorkshireman made five Test appearances for England on the 1963–64 tour of India, scoring 70 runs and taking 9 wickets, but had to wait over six years for his next match, against the Rest of the World at Headingley, when in front of his home crowd he became Eddie Barlow's hat-trick victim?

7. Which man played fifty-four times for Worcestershire before losing an arm in the First World War? Turning to umpiring, he was to stand in a record 48 Test matches between 1924 and 1955.

8. Who, at the age of fifty, played in his twelfth Test for England, against the West Indies in January 1930, a record period of 17 years and 316 days after his previous cap against Australia in March 1912, when one of the West Indies team, Derek Sealy, was not even born?

9. Who, after winning his forty-ninth cap, against the West Indies in February 1968, had to wait almost seven years, a period in which England played sixty-two Tests, before winning his fiftieth, against the full force of Lillee and Thomson in Perth?

10. Who played in his fourth Test for England in June 1963, taking 3 West Indies wickets in four balls, after having played his third Test 11 years and 8 months previously, an intervening period in which England had contested 103 Test matches?

100 *England v. Australia – Test miscellany*

1. Which Australian all-rounder made his Test début in July 1985, falling leg before wicket to Ian Botham off the first ball that he received? Although his batting improved, his bowling tailed off and his figures of 4–114 in this match were followed with 2–373 in the remainder of the series.

2. Who carried his bat for 193* in Australia's total of 383 at Lord's in 1926 and, at 42 years and 201 days, remains the oldest Australian to score a century in an Ashes Test?

3. Who scored four centuries for England in the 1924–25 series against Australia, including three in successive innings?

4. Who was the unfortunate England captain, later to lose his life in a shipwreck, who suffered a 5–0 'whitewash' in the 1920–21 series at the hands of Warwick Armstrong's Australians?

5. Who was the former Everton and England footballer who made his cricketing début for England on the 1920–21 tour of Australia, at thirty-eight years of age, and scored his only Test match century, 117, in the Fourth Test at Melbourne?

6. Which twenty-three-year-old Lymington (Hampshire) born left-arm bowler, domiciled in Queensland, made his début for Australia in the Seventh Test against England at Sydney in February 1971 and, sharing the new ball with Dennis Lillee, had match figures of 5–97 in what was to be his solitary Ashes Test?

7. Who in March 1929 became the oldest player to score a century in a Test match, when, at 46 years and 82 days, he made 142 for England against Australia at Melbourne?

8. Which Australian batsman, in a Test career that spanned twenty-two years from 1890 to 1912, remains the only player to appear in more than fifty Ashes Test matches?

9. Who made his début for Australia against England in March 1925 at thirty-three years of age, and took 106 wickets in twenty-two Ashes Tests prior to August 1934?

10. Which England fast bowler took twenty-one Australian wickets in the 'Bodyline' Test series of 1932–3 without having to resort to this exaggerated form of 'leg-theory'?

101 *1988 – One-day cricket*

1. Who, in Sussex's innings of 182–9 against Middlesex, became the tenth bowler to take a hat-trick in a Benson and Hedges Cup match?

2. Who, playing against Essex, scored a century in the semi-final of the 1988 Benson and Hedges Cup, ensuring a first appearance for his county in a Lord's One-Day Final?

3. Who was the victim of a freak dismissal in the other Benson and Hedges Cup semi-final when, in the act of fending off a rising ball, his glove dislodged his helmet, which rolled onto his stumps?

4. Which minor county beat Northamptonshire in a thrilling finish to a first-round Nat West Trophy match, the winning runs being scored off the final ball, with the last pair at the wicket?

5. Who set a new record for any one-day competition, taking 8–21 in a first-round Nat West Trophy match, figures that would have been even more remarkable had he not been penalised for bowling nine no-balls?

6. Which former first-class county wicket-keeper scored 110 of Cambridgeshire's 173–6 against Warwickshire in a first-round Nat West Trophy match, winning the Man of the Match award, though his side were defeated by 67 runs?

7. Who made his England début in the three-match one-day series against the West Indies?

8. Who, playing in front of his home crowd, won the Man of the Match award in the first One-Day Test, his victims in a 4–31 return being specialist batsmen Gordon Greenidge, Viv Richards, Gus Logie and Carl Hooper?

9. Who averaged 65·00 for England in the four match one-day series in New Zealand, having scored just one run in his only Test innings of the tour?

10. Which veteran left-hander scored the first century of the 1988 Refuge Assurance League, 103* against Surrey, and the following week became the sixth batsman to score 6,000 runs in Sunday League cricket?

102 *1988 – Batting and bowling*

1. Who had bowling figures of 7–16, including a spell of 5–0, when Warwickshire dismissed Cambridge University for 78 in April 1988?

2. During Graeme Hick's mammoth 405* against Somerset, which two players partnered him in record Worcestershire stands for the sixth and eighth wickets, contributing respectively 56 out of 265 and 31* out of an unbroken 177?

3. Which West Indian tourist scored a double century in his first innings of the season in England, having performed the identical feat in 1986?

4. Which Cambridge University undergraduate showed a partiality for capital city bowling attacks in 1988, when scoring 100* against Surrey and a career-best 151* against Middlesex?

5. Who were Worcestershire's opponents when Graeme Hick scored 172 to pass 1,000 first-class runs before the end of May?

6. Which Test bowler returned figures of 7–15 as champions Nottinghamshire were shot out for 44 in June 1988, opener Mike Newell carrying his bat for 10*

7. Which young Surrey bowler achieved a career-best innings return of 9–45 against Cambridge University in June 1988?

8. Who had an innings return of 8–58 for Yorkshire against Essex, the best individual bowling performance for the county since Graham Stevenson's 8–57 against Northamptonshire in 1980?

9. Which forty-seven-year-old claimed his 1,000th first-class victim in 1988, twenty years after his county début?

10. Who became the first bowler in the 1988 English first-class season to attain 50 dismissals, a strike-rate contrasting sharply with his 1987 season, when he finished up with just 15 wickets?

103 1988 – Mixed bag

1. During his return to first-class cricket with Tasmania, who was the former Test opener dismissed by Dennis Lillee with the first ball of his return in January 1988?

2. Who, in January 1988, hit 10 sixes in an innings of 166 for England against Northern Districts in Hamilton, New Zealand?

3. Which West Indian island won the inaugural Red Stripe Cup, the islands' principal domestic competition, previously known as the Shell Shield?

4. Which young fast bowler claimed a record 35 wickets in a West Indian domestic season, an achievement which earned him a test début in the subsequent series against Pakistan?

5. Who, with figures of 8–101, in Queensland's first innings in the 1987/88 Sheffield Shield Final, became only the fifth bowler to claim 50 wickets in the competition in one season?

6. Who, on the opening day of the 1988 English first-class season, completed the unique feat of scoring a century in his maiden innings for two separate counties?

7. Which county was the first to win a four-day Championship match, ironically beating Hampshire by nine wickets with over two days to spare?

8. Which four-day match in April 1988 produced 1,570 runs, a record for the County Championship?

9. Who won the distinction of being Dennis Lillee's first County Championship 'victim' for Northamptonshire?

10. Which cricketer received an MBE in the Queen's Birthday Honours List to gild the reported £52,168 raised by his Benefit?

104 *1988 – Test matches*

1. Who scored 139 for England in the 'Celebration' Bicentennial Test in Sydney, and ended up being fined by the management for sending a stump flying in a rather unfestive fit of pique at the manner of his dismissal?

2. Who saved Australia from the prospect of defeat with an unbeaten 184 in their second innings in the 1988 Bicentennial Test?

3. Who missed out on his maiden Test century when being dismissed for 99 at Eden Park, Auckland, the ninth Englishman to suffer this fate in a Test match?

4. Who scored 107* against England at Eden Park, Auckland, becoming only the fourth New Zealander to score a century on his Test match début?

5. Which specialist batsman also scored 107* for New Zealand against England this time at Wellington, having accumulated only 224 runs at an average of 11.20 in his thirteen previous Test appearances?

6. Who scored England's only century in the 1987/88 three-match Test series against New Zealand?

7. Who was the only England player to make his Test début on the 1987/88 tour of New Zealand?

8. Who was the nineteen-year-old Indian leg-spinner who made an inspired Test début in Madras in January 1988, taking eight West Indies wickets in each innings for record match figures by a débutant of 16–136?

9. Who had match figures of 11–121 when his country recorded a nine-wicket victory over the West Indies at Georgetown, Guyana in April 1988, their first home defeat in Tests for ten years?

10. Who, when scoring 146 at Trent Bridge, registered the first century of the 1988 England against West Indies Test series?

Answers

1 *The 1987 World Cup tournament*
1. Allan Border   2. Graham Gooch   3. Eddie Hemmings
4. David Houghton   5. Vivian Richards   6. Abdul Qadir
7. Sunil Gavaskar   8. Chetan Sharma   9. Craig
McDermott   10. David Boon

2 *Current Players with their second County*
1. John Childs   2. Bill Athey   3. Warwickshire   4. Peter
Willey   5. Kent   6. Chris Broad   7. Eddie Hemmings
8. Trevor Jesty   9. Gehan Mendis   10. Neal Radford

3 *All-Rounders in Test cricket*
1. Kapil Dev   2. Ian Botham   3. Intikhab Alam
4. Mushtaq Mohammad   5. Alan Davidson, Trevor
Goddard and Gary Sobers   6. Alan Davidson   7. Frank
Worrell   8. Ian Johnson   9. Vinoo Mankad   10. George
Giffen (Australia)

4 *Around the Counties*
1. Chris Balderstone (Leicestershire v. Gloucestershire)
2. Nottinghamshire   3. Alan Lewis Jones   4. Jack
Robertson (Middlesex)   5. Gloucestershire   6. Percy
Fender   7. Clive Radley   8. Roland Butcher (Middlesex)
9. Peter Roebuck (Somerset)   10. Trevor Jesty

5 *Test Cricket – Captains*
1.   Clive Lloyd   2. Nawab of Pataudi, Jnr (Mansur Ali
Khan)   3. Abdul Hafeez Kardar   4. John Reid   5. Ali
Bacher   6. Alan Melville   7. Bandula Warnapura
8. Alvin Kallicharan   9. Richie Benaud and Frank
Worrell   10. Duleep Mendis

6 *One-day cricket – The Sunday League*
1. Hampshire   2. Worcestershire   3. Robert Bailey
4. Gordon Greenidge (stand with Chris Smith)   5. Geoff
Holmes   6. Ian Botham   7. Graham Gooch (171) and
Brian Hardie (60) Essex v. Notts at Trent Bridge   8. Keith
Boyce (Essex)   9. Bob Clapp   10. Clive Rice
(Nottinghamshire)

7 England v. Australia – Test match miscellany

1. Chris Broad   2. John Emburey   3. Wayne Phillips
4. David Gower   5. Jeff Thomson   6. Craig McDermott
(901)   7. Ian Botham   8. Graham Dilley   9. Geoffrey
Boycott   10. Mick Malone

8 County Championship captains

1. Roger Knight   2. Colin Cowdrey, Bob Barber, Raman
Subba Row, Ted Dexter and Mike Smith   3. John Barclay
4. Ian Greig   5. Graham Gooch   6. Tom Pearce   7. Tom
Pugh   8. Alan Ealham   9. Brian Close   10. Jack Bond

9 Test match miscellany

1. Chris Tavaré   2. Norman Cowans   3. Dilip Sardesai
4. Dick Lilley (finishing with 84)   5. Wilfred Rhodes
(finishing with 1,706 runs, 109 wickets)   6. Eddie Paynter
(0) and Denis Compton (1)   7. Rodney Redmond   8. Chris
Smith   9. Tony Pigott   10. Salim Malik

10 Cricket records

1. Glenn Turner   2. Zaheer Abbas   3. Graeme Hick
4. Ken Rutherford   5. John Emburey   6. Javed Miandad
and Younis Ahmed   7. Martin Weston   8. Kent
9. Yorkshire   10. Richard Moore (316) and Eddie Paynter
(322)

11 England bowlers

1. Doug Wright   2. Sydney Barnes   3. Ian Peebles
4. Chris Old   5. Ian Botham   6. John Lever   7. Tony
Greig   8. Maurice Tate   9. Fred 'Nutty' Martin
10. George Lohmann

12 Test match batting miscellany

1. Graeme Fowler (201) and Mike Gatting (207)   2. John
Reid   3. Javed Miandad   4. Dennis Amiss   5. Charles
Russell   6. Joe Darling   7. Graeme Wood   8. Allan Border
– 533 in 1981 and 597 in 1985   9. Qasim Omar
10. Keith Stackpole

13 *Transfer trail*
1. Neil Mallender   2. Winston Davis   3. Alastair Storie
4. Allan Jones (he also played for Somerset and Middlesex)
5. David Smith   6. Nick Cook (Northamptonshire ex
Leicestershire)   7. Norman Gifford   8. Alan Ormrod
(Worcestershire 1962–83, before moving to Lancashire)
9. Roger Knight (Surrey 1968–70 and 1978–84,
Gloucestershire 1971–5, Sussex 1976–7)   10. Sydney
Barnes

14 *One-day internationals*
1. Sunil Gavaskar   2. Chris Broad   3. Dean Jones
4. Bruce Reid   5. Simon Davis   6. John Emburey
7. Phillip de Freitas   8. David Gower   9. Ian Botham
10. Vic Marks

15 *Family connections*
1. Chris Smith 217 Hampshire v. Warwickshire and Robin
Smith 209* Hampshire v. Essex   2. George Gunn and
George Vernon Gunn (Nottinghamshire)   3. William Quaife
and William Bernard Quaife and William and Robert
Bestwick   4. Mervyn Harvey (brother of Neil)   5. Syd
Gregory (son of Ned and nephew of Dave)   6. Frank and
Alec Hearne – Frank had previously played for England
against South Africa. The third brother was George, and the
cousin Jack Hearne.   7. John Reid (bowler Bruce)
8. Parks – Jim Senior (J. H.) played in 1 Test 1937, Jim
(J. M.) played in 46 Tests 1954–68, and Bobby kept wicket
for England after Bruce French's injury at Lords 1986.
9. Brendon and John Bracewell   10. Frank Mann – 5
Tests 1922–23, George Mann – 7 Tests, 1948–9

16 *England v. India*
1. Bhagwat Chandrasekhar   2. Peter Parfitt   3. Ken
Barrington   4. Fred Trueman   5. Derek Underwood
6. Peter Lever   7. Tony Lewis   8. Vijay Manjrekar
9. Allan Watkins   10. Mohammad Azharuddin

17 *Derbyshire*
1. Peter Kirsten   2. John Wright   3. Eddie Barlow
4. John Morris   5. Alan Hill (153) and Iain Anderson
(134)   6. George Dawkes   7. Cliff Gladwin   8. Les
Jackson   9. 1936; Arthur Richardson   10. Tommy
Mitchell

18 *Test match captains – England and Australia*
1. Greg Chappell and Tony Greig   2. Ian Botham   3. Bob
Willis, 1982–3   4. Tom Graveney and Barry Jarman
5. Neil Harvey   6. Ian Johnson   7. Bill Woodfull
8. Warwick Armstrong   9. Hon. Frank Jackson and Joe
Darling (21.11.1870)   10. Dave Gregory (Australia) and
James Lillywhite (England)

19 *Prowess in other sports*
1. Philip Horne   2. Ian Greig   3. Graham Barlow
4. Johnny Arnold   5. Harold 'H.G.' Owen-Smith
6. Michael Elgie   7. Edward Wynward   8. Alan Walker
9. Cyril Wilkinson   10. John Wilson

20 *Touring sides against the Counties*
1. Javed Miandad   2. Mudassar Nazar   3. Clive Lloyd
4. Majid Khan   5. Charlie Griffith (West Indies)   6. Bill
Lawry (61.18) and Norman O'Neill (60.03)   7. Jackie
McGlew   8. Hugh Tayfield   9. Arthur Morris   10. Bill
Johnston

21 *Essex*
1. Graham Gooch   2. Neil Foster   3. David East – as a
wicket-keeper he took 8 catches in Somerset's first innings,
equalling a record originally set by Wally Grout for
Queensland against Western Australia in 1960   4. 1979
5. Trevor Bailey   6. Barry Knight   7. Ken McEwan
8. Lee Irvine   9. Johnny 'J.W.H.T' Douglas   10. Percy
Perrin

22 *One-day cricket – The Sunday League*
1. Greg Chappell (for Somerset)   2. Lancashire
3. Richard Hutton   4. Alan Ward   5. Brian Langford
(Somerset)   6. Worcestershire   7. Middlesex   8. Glenn
Turner   9. Dennis Amiss   10. Somerset

23 *Career statistics – Wicket-keepers*
1. John Murray   2. George Dawkes   3. David Bairstow
4. Barrie Meyer   5. David Hunter   6. Harold
Stephenson   7. Leslie Ames   8. Fred Huish   9. Jimmy
Binks   10. Deryck Murray

24 *Christian names*
1. John AUGUSTINE Snow   2. Peter BARKER Howard
May   3. Nicholas Grant BILLSON Cook   4. Robert George
DYLAN Willis   5. Philippe HENRI Edmonds   6. Michael
John KNIGHT Smith   7. Christopher LYALL Smith
8. Roland ORLANDO Butcher   9. Frederick SEWARDS
Trueman   10. Anthony Charles SHACKLETON Pigott

25 *Glamorgan*
1. Matthew Maynard   2. Hugh Morris   3. Alan Jones
4. Wilfred Wooller   5. Allan Watkins   6. Don Shepherd
7. Peter Walker   8. John 'J.C.' Clay   9. Paul Todd
10. Rodney Ontong and John Steele

26 *Test match grounds*
1. Melbourne (Australia v. England, December 1970 and
January 1971)   2. Bramall Lane, Sheffield   3. Kingsmead,
Durban   4. Chidambaram Stadium, Madras
5. Wellington, New Zealand   6. Ahmedabad
7. Johannesburg – Old Wanderers, Ellis Park and
Wanderers Stadium, Bombay – Gymkhana Ground,
Brabourne Stadium and Wankhede Stadium   8. Durban
(1910–21, before being replaced by Kingsmead)   9. Jackie
Hampshire   10. George Headley

27 *Test cricket – Not England*
1. Simpson Guillen   2. Dudley Nourse   3. Patrick
Lashley   4. Ian Meckiff   5. Godfrey Lawrence   6. Peter
Toohey   7. Barry Sinclair   8. Les Favell   9. Majid Khan
(Pakistan v. New Zealand)   10. Gary Gilmour

28 *England v. Australia – Test match miscellany*
1. Phil Edmonds   2. Peter Lever   3. John Edrich
4. Dennis Amiss   5. Bob Massie   6. Tom Cartwright
7. John Snow   8. Derek Underwood   9. John Inverarity
10. John Edrich

29 *Gloucestershire*
1. Zaheer Abbas   2. Mike Procter against Essex in 1972
and Yorkshire in 1979   3. Tony Brown   4. Wally
Hammond   5. John Mortimore   6. Arthur Milton
7. Charlie Parker   8. Gilbert Jessop   9. Mark Alleyne
10. George Emmett

30 *One-day internationals*
1. Viv Richards   2. Allan Lamb   3. Phillip de Freitas
4. Graham Marsh (104) and David Boon (111): Australia
(250–3) lost to India (251–3) by 7 wickets   5. Javed
Miandad (Pakistan)   6. Bill Athey   7. Graham Gooch
8. Joel Garner   9. Desmond Haynes   10. Zaheer Abbas

31 *University cricket*
1. Michael Atherton   2. Mark Crawley   3. Paul Bail
4. Giles Toogood   5. Robin Boyd-Moss   6. Paul Parker
7. Mike Smith   8. Nawab of Pataudi, Jnr   9. John Dewes
(204*) and Hubert Doggart (219*)   10. Roger Prideaux
and Tony Lewis

32 *Australian cricket*
1. Victoria (v. New South Wales)   2. Don Bradman
3. Bill Ponsford   4. Alan Kippax 260* and Hal Hooker
62   5. John Inverarity   6. Tony Lock   7. Garfield
Sobers   8. David Hookes   9. Mike Veletta   10. Colin
Milburn

33 *Hampshire*
1. Gordon Greenidge   2. Barry Richards   3. Peter
Sainsbury   4. Derek Shackleton   5. Phil Mead   6. Hon.
Lionel Tennyson (grandson of the poet)   7. Andy Roberts
8. Colin Ingleby-Mackenzie   9. David Turner   10. Paul
Terry (with Chris Smith and Gordon Greenidge
respectively)

34 *Test match batting miscellany*
1. Graham Yallop   2. Andy Roberts   3. Seymour Nurse
4. Mike Gatting   5. Winston Davis   6. John Beck
7. Herbert Sutcliffe   8. Chetan Chauhan   9. Mudassar
Nazar   10. Kepler Wessels

35 *Hundreds*
1. Allan Lamb   2. John Langridge   3. John Carr
(Middlesex) and Matthew Maynard (Glamorgan)   4. Alan
Lilley (Essex)   5. Denis Compton in 1947   6. Jack Hobbs
7. Charles 'C.B.' Fry   8. John Langridge   9. Colin
McDonald (127), Neil Harvey (204), Keith Miller (109),
Ron Archer (128) and Richie Benaud (121)   10. Clyde
Walcott

36 *West Indies batsmen*
1. Robert Christiani   2. Alvin Kallicharran   3. Gordon
Greenidge   4. Frank Worrell   5. Everton Weekes: against
England (141 at Sabina Park, March 1948) and against
India (128 at Delhi, November 1948, 194 at Bombay, 162
and 101 at Calcutta and 90 at Madras, January 1949)
6. Lawrence Rowe   7. Clifford Roach   8. George
Headley   9. Rohan Kanhai   10. Conrad Hunte

37 *Kent*
1. Derek Underwood   2. Terry Alderman   3. Richard
Ellison   4. Colin Cowdrey   5. Arthur Fagg   6. William
Henry Ashdown (his county career, however, stretched only
from 1920 to 1937)   7. Alfred Percy 'Tich' Freeman
8. Colin Blythe   9. Norman Graham   10. Derek Aslett

38 *England v. Australia – Test miscellany*
1. Les Ames   2. Billy Murdoch   3. Jack Hobbs
4. Herbert Sutcliffe   5. Clem Hill (Australia)   6. Dennis
Lillee – 8,516 balls and 167 wickets (1 wicket every 51
balls).   7. Wilfred Rhodes   8. Pat Pocock   9. Gubby Allen
and Bill Voce   10. Arthur Chipperfield

39 *England v. New Zealand*
1. Jeff Crowe   2. Tony MacGibbon   3. Lance Cairns
4. Richard Hadlee   5. Ken Barrington   6. Bevan Congdon
and Vic Pollard   7. Mark Burgess and Geoff Boycott
8. Richard Collinge   9. Martin Donnelly   10. Bob
Appleyard

40 *The Prudential World Cup*
1. Martin Snedden   2. Pakistan   3. David Hookes
4. India   5. Winston Davis   6. Trevor Chappell   7. Kapil
Dev   8. Mohinder Amarnath   9. Duncan Fletcher
10. Ian Gould

41 *Lancashire*
1. David Hughes   2. Neil Fairbrother   3. David Green
4. Ken Grieves   5. Warren Hegg   6. Ted McDonald
7. Archie McLaren   8. Peter Lee   9. Leonard Green
10. Ian Folley

42 *England batsmen*
1. John Emburey   2. Bob Woolmer   3. Wally Hammond:
251 and 200 v. Australia 1928–9, and 227 and 336* v.
New Zealand 1932–3   4. Andy Sandham (England v. West
Indies, April 1930)   5. Colin Cowdrey   6. Mickey
Stewart   7. John Edrich and Ken Barrington (Surrey)
8. Eddie Paynter – 216* at Trent Bridge in June 1938 and
243 at Durban in January 1939   9. Ken Barrington
10. Denis Compton

43 *Career statistics – Bowlers*
1. Dr Rudi Webster   2. Bob Appleyard (Yorkshire)
3. Kevin Jarvis   4. John Warr   5. Bill Bowes (Yorkshire)
6. Roy Tattersall (Lancashire)   7. Derek Shackleton 1949–
68 (career 1948–69)   8. Tom Goddard   9. Hedley
Verity   10. Tony Cordle

44 *Test match bowling miscellany*
1. Sarfraz Nawaz   2. Arnold Sidebottom   3. Doug
Wright   4. Leslie 'Chuck' Fleetwood-Smith   5. Arthur
Mailey   6. Chetan Sharma   7. Greg Matthews   8. Abdul
Qadir   9. Maninder Singh   10. Ian Botham

45 *Leicestershire*
1. Nigel Briers   2. Jonathan Agnew   3. 1975   4. Jack
van Geloven   5. Maurice Hallam   6. Ken Higgs
7. Roger Tolchard   8. Cecil 'C.J.B.' Wood   9. George
Geary   10. Ray Illingworth and Ken Higgs

46 Benson and Hedges Cup
1. Andy Stovold 2. Chris Old 3. Graham McKenzie
4. David Thomas 5. Phil Sharpe 6. Colin Cowdrey
7. For the first time the Combined Universities team was
drawn from all British universities, not just Oxford and
Cambridge. 8. Peter Roebuck and Martin Crowe
9. Winston Benjamin 10. Allan Lamb
(Northamptonshire)

47 Test match miscellany
1. Roy Dias 2. Martin Crowe 3. Andy Lloyd 4. Pat
Pocock 5. Bhagwat Chandrasekhar 6. Eddie
Hemmings 7. Wilfred Rhodes 8. Eknath Solkar
9. Denis Atkinson 10. New Zealand

48 England v. Australia – Test match miscellany
1. Bob Barber 2. Bob Cowper 3. Geoff Boycott
4. Bobby Simpson (311) 5. Ken Barrington 6. Tom
Veivers 7. Neil Hawke 8. Graham McKenzie 9. Richie
Benaud 10. Alec Bedser

49 Middlesex
1. Wilf Slack – the other double centurions being Javed
Miandad (Glamorgan) and Andy Sandham (Surrey)
2. Eric Russell 3. Mike Selvey 4. Vintcent Van der Bijl
5. Fred Titmus 6. Jack Robertson 7. Elias 'Patsy'
Hendren 8. Peter Parfitt 9. Leslie Compton 10. Colin
Drybrough

50 Test match batting miscellany
1. Len Hutton 2. Gary Cosier (109) v. West Indies
3. Allan Border 4. Zaheer Abbas 5. Motganhalli
Jaisimha 6. Nazar Mohammad (124* at Lucknow,
October 1952) and Mudassar Nazar (152* at Lahore,
January 1983) 7. Mike Smith 8. John Edrich (310* v.
New Zealand at Headingley in 1965) 9. Mohinder
Amarnath (India) 10. Wayne Phillips

51 Former players with more than one county
1. David Green 2. Surrey 3. Brian Bolus 4. Bob
Berry 5. Hampshire 6. Essex 7. Bob Wyatt
8. Leicestershire 9. Raman Subba Row 10. Peter
Richardson

52 *England all-rounders*
1. Chris Cowdrey 2. The Right Hon. Sir Francis Stanley Jackson 3. Maurice Tate 4. Richard Hutton 5. Fred Titmus 6. Wally Hammond 7. Barry Knight 8. George 'Gubby' Allen 9. Gilbert Jessop 10. Basil d'Oliveira

53 *Northamptonshire*
1. Roger Harper 2. Robert Bailey 3. Alastair Storie 4. David Steele 5. Roy Virgin, Jim Watts and Mushtaq Mohammad 6. George Tribe 7. Mushtaq Mohammad 8. Raman Subba Row (it was against his former county) 9. Geoff Cook 10. Gloucestershire

54 *Test match miscellany*
1. Taslim Arif 2. Rodney Marsh 3. Mike Brearley (1978–9) 4. Graham Yallop 5. Faoud Bacchus 6. Geoff Boycott 7. Desmond Haynes 8. Roland Butcher 9. Terry Alderman 10. Keith Fletcher

55 *One-day cricket – The Sunday League*
1. Derek Underwood and John Lever 2. Jack Simmons 3. Sussex 4. David Thomas 5. Roger Tolchard 6. John Steele 101 (Leicestershire and Glamorgan) 7. Barry Richards (Hampshire) 8. Surrey (304–6) and Warwickshire (300–9) at The Oval 9. Graham Gooch (116) and Ken McEwan (162*) for Essex 10. Bob Taylor

56 *Australian tours to England*
1. Kerry O'Keeffe 2. Keith Stackpole 3. Charles Macartney 4. Bill Johnston 5. Surrey 6. Colin McCool 7. Clarrie Grimmett 8. Victor Trumper 9. Charles Turner 10. Don Bradman (89.92), Lindsay Hassett (74.42), Arthur Morris (71.18), Bill Brown (57.92), Sam Loxton (57.23), Sid Barnes (56.41) and Neil Harvey (53.76)

57 *Nottinghamshire*
1. Mick Newell 2. Richard Hadlee 3. Cleethorpes 4. Mike Smedley 5. Carlton Forbes 6. Bruce Dooland 7. Geoff Millman 8. George and John Gunn 9. Harold Larwood 10. Arthur Carr

58 *England v. Australia – Test match miscellany*
1. Sidney Barnes (234) 2. Bill Bowes 3. Jim Laker
4. Len Hutton 5. Eric Hollies 6. Reg Simpson
7. Arthur Morris 8. Grahame Corling 9. Trevor Bailey
10. Ian Meckiff

59 *University cricket*
1. Roger Moulding 2. Stephen Wookey 3. Ashley
Harvey-Walker and John Whitehouse 4. Esmond
Kentish 5. Sussex 6. Norman Mitchell-Innes 7. Tony
Pearson 8. Robin Marlar 9. Paul Gibb 10. Dick Lowe

60 *Test cricket firsts – Batting*
1. Abbas Ali Baig (India) 2. Geoff Boycott 3. Norman
Yardley 4. Gundappa Viswanath 5. Herbert Sutcliffe
6. Charles Macartney 7. Seymour Nurse 8. Russell
Endean 9. Peter Willey 10. Roshan Shodhan

61 *Somerset*
1. High Wycombe (Buckinghamshire) 2. Martin Crowe
3. Peter Roebuck 4. Vivian Richards 5. Ian Botham
6. Graham Atkinson 7. Harold Gimblett 8. Jack 'J.C.'
White 9. Harold Stephenson 10. John Daniell

62 *England v. Pakistan*
1. Sikander Bakht 2. Jim McConnon 3. Khalid Hassan
4. Neil Foster 5. Vic Marks 6. Asif Iqbal 7. Zaheer
Abbas 8. Derek Underwood 9. Peter Parfitt 10. He
was dismissed for a 'pair' within two hours on the third
afternoon of the match. Johnny Wardle had a hand in both
dismissals, having him caught by David Sheppard in the
first innings and catching him off Alec Bedser in the second.

63 *Gillette Cup/NatWest Trophy*
1. Devon 2. Alan Dixon (7–15 v. Surrey, 1967)
3. Simon Davis 4. Clive Radley 5. Gehan Mendis
6. Bishen Bedi 7. Alan Knott 8. Lincolnshire 9. David
Larter 10. Geoff Robinson

64 *Gentlemen v. Players*
1. 1962 2. Ted Dexter and Fred Trueman 3. Eddie
Craig and Ossie Wheatley 4. David Pithey 5. Freddie
Brown 6. Alex Kennedy 7. Ian Peebles 8. Wally
Hammond 9. Jack Hobbs 10. Charles 'C.B.' Fry

65 *Surrey*
1. David Ward   2. Robin Jackman   3. Sylvester Clarke
4. Pat Pocock   5. Stuart Surridge   6. Percy Fender
7. Herbert Strudwick   8. Tom Hayward   9. Tom
Richardson   10. Bobby Abel

66 *England v. Australia – Test match miscellany*
1. Jim Laker 4–75 and Tony Lock 5–45 (James de Courcy
was run out)   2. Norman O'Neill   3. Colin McDonald
4. Cyril Washbrook   5. The Reverend David Sheppard
6. Alan Oakman   7. Charles Barnett   8. Denis Compton
9. Stan McCabe   10. Joe Hardstaff, Jnr

67 *Career statistics – All-rounders*
1. Brian Close   2. Frank Woolley   3. George Hirst
4. Billy Ibadulla (Pakistan)   5. Freddie Brown   6. Mike
Procter   7. Trevor Bailey (28,642 and 2,082), Ray
Illingworth (24,134 and 2,072) and Fred Titmus (21,588
and 2,830)   8. Stewart Storey (Surrey and Sussex)
9. George Hirst and Wilfred Rhodes (from Kirkheaton)
10. Alex Kennedy and Jack Newman

68 *England Captains*
1. Mike Brearley (1977–81)   2. Ian Botham (1980–81)
3. Brian Close   4. Tony Lewis   5. Colin Cowdrey
6. Peter May   7. Donald Carr   8. Wally Hammond
9. Archie MacLaren   10. Bob Wyatt

69 *Sussex*
1. Colin and Alan Wells who scored 140* and 161*
respectively   2. James and John Langridge   3. Arthur and
Harold Gilligan   4. John Spencer   5. Geoff Arnold, Arnold
Long and Stewart Storey   6. Ian Thomson   7. Alan
Melville   8. Maurice Tate   9. George Cox, Snr
10. Kumar Ranjitsinhji

70 *Gillette Cup/NatWest Trophy*
1. Hugh Morris (Glamorgan)   2. Martin Jean-Jacques
3. Dermot Reeve (Sussex)   4. Alvin Kallicharan
(Warwickshire)   5. Joel Garner   6. Garfield Sobers (1968–
74)   7. Geoff Arnold (Surrey to 1978, then Sussex)
8. Jack Bond   9. Geoff Boycott   10. Peter Marner

71 *High scores – Individual*
1. Kumar Ranjitsinhji 2. John Jameson 3. Zaheer
Abbas 4. Len Hutton 5. Colin Cowdrey 6. Lawrence
Rowe (for West Indies against New Zealand at Sabina Park,
Kingston, Jamaica) 7. Don Bradman 8. Kumar
Duleepsinhji 9. Reg 'R.E.' Foster 10. Dilip Vengsarkar

72 *England v. South Africa*
1. Arthur Gilligan and Maurice Tate 2. Bruce Mitchell
3. Colin Bland 4. Brian Statham and Ken Higgs 5. Ken
Barrington 6. Alec Bedser 7. Bill Edrich 8. Eric
Rowan 9. Peter May 10. Norman 'Tufty' Mann

73 *Warwickshire*
1. Gordon Lord 2. Geoff Humpage 3. Jim Stewart
4. Eric Hollies 5. Tom Cartwright 6. Willie Quaife
7. Tom Pritchard 8. Arthur 'Dick' Lilley 9. Frank
Foster 10. Harry Howell

74 Test match bowling miscellany
1. Dennis Lillee 2. 'Bapu' Nadkarni 3. Lance Cairns
4. Clarrie Grimmett 5. Carl Rackemann 6. Kapil Dev
7. Nick Cook 8. Laxman Sivaramakrishnan 9. Craig
McDermott 10. Wazsim Akram

75 *Christian names*
1. Lawrence BARNARD Fishlock 2. John David BENBOW
Robertson 3. Stewart CATHIE Griffith (Billy) 4. Norman
Walter DRANSFIELD Yardley 5. Maurice FLETCHER
Tremlett 6. Frank HOLMES Tyson 7. Christopher
MIDDLETON Old 8. Douglas Vivian PARSON Wright
9. Richard THOMPSON Spooner (Dick) 10. Clive
THORNTON Radley

76 *Benson and Hedges Cup*
1. Jim Love (Yorkshire) 2. Somerset (This action
rebounded on them when they were expelled from the 1979
competition by the TCCB) 3. John Abrahams 4. Viv
Richards 5. John Emburey (Middlesex) 6. Scotland
7. Martyn Moxon 93* and Ashley Metcalfe 94* for
Yorkshire) 8. Essex 9. Roger Knight (Surrey) 10. Ken
Higgs

77 Worcestershire
1. Richard Illingworth   2. Graeme Hick   3. Neal
Radford   4. Glenn Turner   5. Don Kenyon   6. Martin
Horton   7. Roly Jenkins   8. Roy Booth   9. Derek 'Dick'
Richardson   10. Syd Buller

78 England v. Australia – Test match miscellany
1. George 'Gubby' Allen   2. Jack Fingleton (136) and Don
Bradman (270)   3. Bill Ponsford   4. Bill Woodfull
5. Harold Larwood   6. The Nawab of Pataudi, Snr
7. Percy Chapman   8. Bert Ironmonger   9. Harold
Larwood   10. Archie Jackson

79 Cricket records
1. David Bairstow (Yorkshire)   2. Steve O'Shaughnessy
3. Lancashire (166–0 dec. and 66–0) beat Leicestershire
(108 and 122)   4. Essex (ironically this was the only time
the tourists were bowled out in a county match during the
season)   5. Wally Hammond   6. Leslie Ames   7. Keith
Andrew (Northants)   8. Middlesex (Jack Hearne and Harry
Lee scored centuries in both games)   9. Hampshire
10. Northamptonshire

80 Gillette Cup/NatWest Trophy finals – The players
1. Roy Virgin (Somerset and Northamptonshire)   2. Tim
Lamb (Middlesex and Northamptonshire)   3. David Steel
(Northamptonshire and Derbyshire)   4. John Dye (Kent
and Northamptonshire)   5. Graham Barlow and Clive
Radley   6. Fred Rumsey (Somerset and Derbyshire)
7. Roger Knight (Gloucestershire and Surrey)   8. Tom
Cartwright (Warwickshire and Glamorgan)   9. Bob
Taylor   10. Barry Wood (Lancashire and Derbyshire)

81 Yorkshire
1. Ashley Metcalfe   2. Paul Jarvis   3. Martyn Moxon
4. Ray Illingworth   5. Don Wilson   6. Jimmy Binks
7. Hedley Verity   8. Wilfred Rhodes   9. Herbert Sutcliffe
and Hedley Verity   10. Lord Hawke

82 Test batting – General
1. Sidath Wettimuny 2. Jack Fingleton 3. Dilip
Sardesai 4. Polly Umrigar 5. Graham Yallop – 268 at
Adelaide 6. Leslie Ames 7. Roy Fredericks 8. Wally
Hammond 9. Brendan Kuruppu 10. Ken Eastwood

83 Domestic cricket abroad
1. Allan Lamb 2. Stephen Jefferies 3. David Hookes
4. Rhaguram Bhat 5. Rodney Marsh (Western
Australia) 6. David Hookes (306*) and Wayne Phillips
(213*) 7. Barry Richards (356 South Australia v.
Western Australia 1970–1) 8. Denis Compton 9. Bill
Ponsford 10. Peter Allan

84 The Prudential World Cup
1. Dennis Amiss 2. Glenn Turner 3. Alan Turner
4. Gary Gilmour 5. Clive Lloyd 6. Mike Denness
7. Rohan Kanhai 8. Canada 9. Collis King 10. Joel
Garner

85 County grounds
1. Tunbridge Wells (Kent v. Worcestershire)
2. Hampshire (Basingstoke) 3. New Road, Worcester
4. Warwickshire (Nuneaton) 5. Northamptonshire
6. Taunton 7. Blackheath 8. St Helen's, Swansea
9. Leyton 10. Colchester

86 England v. Australia
1. Denis Compton and Arthur Morris 2. Peter Taylor
3. Maurice Leyland 4. Raman Subba Row 5. John
Blackham 6. Billy Midwinter (8 matches for Australia,
1876–87 and 4 matches for England, 1881–2) 7. Clem
Hill 8. Arthur Mailey (9–121 at Melbourne February
1921) 9. David Steele 10. Doug Walters

87 Career statistics – Batsmen
1. Alan Jones (Glamorgan) 2. Roy Marshall (Barbados
and Hampshire) 3. Philip Mead (Hampshire) 4. David
Gower (August 1986) 5. Tom Graveney 6. Wally
Hammond (50,551 between 1920 and 1951) 7. Tony
Lock 8. Geoff Boycott 9. Frank Woolley 10. Ken
Suttle

88 *Benson and Hedges Cup Finals — The players*
1. Alan Ormrod (Worcestershire and Lancashire)   2. Alan Butcher (Surrey) and Ian Butcher (Leicestershire)
3. Graham Clinton (Kent and Surrey)   4. Paul Downton (Kent and Middlesex)   5. Brian Brain (Worcestershire and Gloucestershire)   6. Christopher and Graham Cowdrey (Kent)   7. Jim Yardley (Worcestershire and Northamptonshire)   8. Norman Gifford (Worcestershire and Warwickshire)   9. Mike Hendrick (Derbyshire and Nottinghamshire)   10. Mike Denness (Kent and Essex)

89 *Around the counties*
1. Hugo Yarnold (Worcestershire)   2. Dick Howorth
3. Winston Davis   4. Younis Ahmed (Surrey, Worcestershire and Glamorgan)   5. Trevor Jesty   6. Jim Griffiths   7. Nick Falkner and Keith Medlycott   8. Derek Underwood   9. Essex   10. Chris Old (Warwickshire)

90 *Wicket-keepers in Test cricket*
1. Ian Smith   2. Bruce French, Bill Athey, Bob Taylor and Bobby Parks   3. Denis Lindsay   4. Les Ames (1950)
5. Bert Oldfield   6. Wally Grout   7. Gil Langley
8. Frank Woolley   9. Bevan Congdon   10. Herbert Strudwick

91 *England v. Australia*
1. Wally Hammond   2. Tom Richardson   3. Bob Willis
4. Geoff Lawson   5. Arthur Morris   6. Kepler Wessels
7. Craig McDermott   8. David Gower (215 at Edgbaston in August 1985)   9. Alf Coxon   10. Wally Hammond

92 *Hat-tricks*
1. Mike Denness (the England twelfth man, fielding as a substitute for the other side)   2. Bob Woolmer   3. Ray East   4. Jimmy Matthews   5. Bob Crisp   6. Richard Hadlee   7. Hugh Trumble   8. Geoff Griffin   9. Mike Procter (Gloucestershire)   10. Maurice Allom

93 *County Championship – Best bowling*
1. Ken Smales 2. Hedley Verity (both times at Headingley) 3. Tony Gray (Surrey) 4. Imran Khan (Sussex) 5. Phillip de Freitas (Leicestershire) 6. Graham McKenzie 7. Ray Illingworth 8. Percy 'Tich' Freeman 9. Bruce Dooland 10. Colin Blythe

94 *Australian cricket*
1. Bill Ponsford 2. Clarrie Grimmett 3. Arthur Mailey 4. Don Tallon 5. Barry Richards 6. John Inverarity 7. Queensland 8. Jack Simmons 9. Charles Turner 10. South Australia

95 *Miscellaneous tours*
1. Bob Taylor, Norman Gifford and Richard Hutton 2. Michael Atherton 3. Freddie Brown 4. Mark Ramprakesh 5. Canada 6. Mike Gatting 7. Eddie Hemmings 8. Maurice Tate 9. Kepler Wessels 10. Peter Kirsten

96 *One-day internationals*
1. Graham Gooch 2. Viv Richards 3. Michael Holding 4. India 5. Allan Border and Dean Jones 6. Javed Miandad 7. Bill Lawry 8. Dennis Amiss (103) against Australia 9. Roy Fredericks 10. Ken Wadsworth

97 *Overseas players in the County Championship*
1. Nottinghamshire 2. Mick Malone 3. Bill Alley (who umpired his first Test match, England v. India, in July 1974 and was called upon to give Sunil Gavaskar out first ball of the match) 4. Leonard 'Jock' Livingston 5. Bruce Francis 6. Derbyshire 7. Sid O'Linn 8. Larry Gomes 9. Lancashire 10. Collis King

98 *Family connections*
1. Paul Sheahan 2. Chris Cowdrey 3. Victor Richardson 4. Ashok Mankad 5. Javed Burki 6. Dave and Dudley Nourse 7. Shoaib Mohammad (son of Hanif) 8. It was the first time that Mudassar Nazar and Shoaib Mohammad had opened the innings together for their country, as their respective fathers, Nazar Mohammad and Hanif Mohammad, had done thirty-two years earlier. 9. Brian Crump 10. Neil Lenham (son of Les)

99 *Test Cricket – Mixed bag*
1. Jack Birkenshaw   2. Younis Ahmed (Pakistan)
3. Sunil Gavaskar (so bringing to an end his record of 106
consecutive Test matches for India)   4. Bob Taylor
5. Ranjan Madugalle   6. Don Wilson   7. Frank Chester
8. George Gunn   9. Fred Titmus   10. Derek Shackleton

100 *England v. Australia – Test match miscellany*
1. Simon O'Donnell   2. Warren Bardsley   3. Herbert
Sutcliffe   4. Johnny 'J.W.H.T.' Douglas   5. Harry
Makepeace   6. Tony Dell   7. Jack Hobbs   8. Syd Gregory
– 58 Tests (52 v. England and 6 v. South Africa)
9. Clarrie Grimmett   10. George 'Gubby' Allen

101 *1988 – One-day cricket*
1. Angus Fraser   2. Paul Terry (Hampshire)   3. Matthew
Maynard (Glamorgan v. Derbyshire)   4. Cheshire
5. Michael Holding (Derbyshire v. Sussex)   6. Mike
Garnham   7. Monte Lynch   8. Gladstone Small   9. Neil
Fairbrother   10. David Turner (Hampshire)

102 *1988 – Batting and bowling*
1. Gordon Parsons   2. Steven Rhodes and Richard
Illingworth 3. Roger Harper (217* v. Sussex)   4. Michael
Atherton   5. The West Indies   6. Gladstone Small
(Warwickshire)   7. Martin Bicknell   8. Stuart Fletcher
9. Jack Simmons (Lancashire)   10. Kevin Cooper
(Nottinghamshire)

103 *1988 – Mixed bag*
1. Andrew Hilditch (South Australia)   2. Tim Robinson
3. Jamaica   4. Curtley Ambrose (Leeward Islands)
5. Chris Matthews (Western Australia)   6. Peter Bowler
(155* for Derbyshire, having scored 100* for Leicestershire in
1986)   7. Surrey   8. Essex v. Kent at Chelmsford (Essex
won by 8 wickets)   9. Andy Stovold (Gloucestershire)
10. John Wright (Derbyshire and New Zealand)

104 *1988 – Test matches*
1. Chris Broad   2. David Boon   3. Martyn Moxon
4. Mark Greatbatch   5. Ken Rutherford   6. Chris Broad
(114 in Christchurch)   7. Paul Jarvis   8. Narendra
Hirwani   9. Imran Khan (Pakistan)   10. Graham Gooch